Working ethically

Working ethically . . . on a Shoestring

Creating a sustainable business without breaking the bank

A & C Black • London

First published in Great Britain 2007

A & C Black Publishers Ltd
38 Soho Square, London W1D 3HB
www.acblack.com

British Library Cataloguing in Publication Data
A CIP record for this book is available from the British Library.

ISBN: 978-0-7136-7548-1

This book is produced using paper that is made from wood grown
in managed, sustainable forests. It is natural, renewable and
recyclable. The logging and manufacturing processes conform to
the environmental regulations of the country of origin.

Design by Fiona Pike, Pike Design, Winchester
Typeset by RefineCatch Limited, Bungay, Suffolk
Printed in Italy by Rotolito

CONTENTS

ABOUT THE AUTHORS

Lorenza Clifford has a master's degree in occupational psychology, a coaching qualification and over ten years' experience of coaching blue-chip clients at all levels of the organisation.

Tim Hindle is the former management editor of *The Economist*.

Nick Kettles is a freelance writer and brand consultant (www.nickkettles.co.uk).

Carry Somers is founder and owner of Pachacuti (www.pachacuti.com), which sells contemporary Fairtrade fashion. She holds a master's degree in Native American studies.

Lesley Somers is founder of The Flame Tree, a Fairtrade enterprise which operates in the UK and Ghana.

The Publishers gratefully acknowledge the help received from the British Association for Fair Trade Shops (BAFTS) during the compilation of this book. For more information, please visit **www.bafts.org.uk**

INTRODUCTION
Tim Hindle

In the era of Gordon Gekko, back in the late 1980s when corporate greed was 'good', most people thought ethical business was an oxymoron. The two, ethics and business, were assumed to mix about as comfortably as oil and water. In the past two decades, however, a remarkable transformation has taken place. Businessmen (and more particularly businesswomen) have been gradually demonstrating that the two can indeed mix, and can sometimes do so very successfully.

Companies such as Body Shop, Starbucks and Linda McCartney's vegetarian foods have led the way. Linda's daughter Stella followed in her mother's footsteps by decreeing that her own high-fashion business would use neither fur nor leather in its garments. Now the big boys are joining in. Body Shop was bought in 2006 by the French cosmetics giant L'Oréal, and Linda McCartney's brand was taken over by Heinz in the same year.

A few companies are going beyond mere recognition that business and ethics can mix. The chief executive of Unilever, a hard-hearted purveyor of soap, spinach and a thousand other consumer goods, has declared that being socially and environmentally responsible 'in the future . . . will be the only way to do business'. In other words, not being pro-actively ethical will, quite simply, be bad for business.

When companies talk about being ethical, however, it is not always clear what they are referring to. Currently to the fore is the idea that the goods and/or services that they sell be produced in a way that is not only profitable but also socially and environmentally responsible – the three sources of the so-called 'triple bottom line' of people, profits and planet. This sort of ethics includes assurances that a company's production processes do not 'exploit' workers in developing countries, for example, do not harm animals (in the testing of chemicals or medicines, for instance) and do not unsustainably consume the environment that we all live in (through indiscriminate logging or excessive use of hydrocarbons).

This focus follows more than a decade in which cost-cutting was the Number 1 priority for business. There has been a gradual reaction against the hidden 'costs' that such a strategy has been perceived to impose. While the retail price of garments and shoes, for example, has fallen in real terms in most rich western countries, this has only been brought about by the switch of manufacturing to low-wage developing countries where labour markets are unregulated and manufacturers are able to ride roughshod over social and environmental standards. Growing awareness of this among consumers has forced companies, including Nike and Tesco, to re-examine their sourcing policies and to keep a closer eye on the ethical standards of suppliers in places as far apart as Mexico and Bangladesh.

Led by the Fairtrade movement, which adds its brand to products that have been produced and traded in an environmentally and socially 'fair' way (and, of course, that concept is open to interpretation), more and more consumers have become aware of the power that they have in their pocket to change things. From small beginnings, the movement has picked up steam in the past five years. In the UK, *Ethical Consumer* magazine, which attempts to be a sort of *Which?* for the ethical movement, has already produced over 100 issues.

Nevertheless, the Fairtrade movement is still only small – focused essentially on coffee, tea, bananas and cotton, and accounting for less than 0.2% of all UK grocery sales in 2006. The leading UK corporate sponsor of this sort of ethical business is the Co-operative Group, a medium-sized retailer concentrated in the north of England. It says that 'climate change, sound sourcing, animal welfare, and waste and packaging' are central to its business.

It is not just consumers who are driving this change. To some extent, companies are also being influenced by the fact that young people are increasingly concerned to work for firms that pay attention to the triple bottom line (people, planet and profits). On top of which, there is a niche market in ethical investing: putting money only into companies which follow certain ethical guidelines. But ethical investing, too, is still small. In the UK, it accounts for just 1% of all retail investment funds. Ethical investing needs to prove that it can produce superior returns before it can attract a more sizeable flow of money.

Much of the growth in ethical business has been market-driven: it has happened because consumers, employers and investors want it. But it is unlikely to take off in any really significant way until governments become more involved. Until now, they have stood on the sidelines, but concerns about global warming are persuading more of them to steer consumption – by means of taxes and/or subsidies – towards environmentally friendly options. With new legislation and regulation in this area, consumer behaviour may begin to change far more dramatically in the not-too-distant future.

The ethical firm

The more traditional meaning of business ethics is that of ethical behaviour within the corporation. This is about firms not bribing customers to secure business, not fiddling accounts to avoid tax, and not backdating stock options to increase managers' rewards.

In the early years of this century, following the WorldCom and Enron scandals in America, where corruption at the top literally destroyed huge corporations and (along with them) the pensions and livelihoods of tens of thousands of people, corporations were forced by government legislation to look more carefully at their 'governance', at the way they ran themselves, and the checks and balances that were in place to prevent internal unethical behaviour. The change was not confined to America. In 1986, just 18% of Britain's larger companies had an internal code of ethics; by 2006 that figure had risen to over 90%.

One reason that companies are increasingly keen to be seen to be clean is that they see themselves as engaged in a 'war for talent', competing for a limited supply of capable young people. And these talented people, they believe, increasingly want to work in places where they can feel good about what they do for most of the day. What's more, in today's knowledge-based businesses, these young people are far more aware of their working environment, of 'what's going on around here', than were their grandfathers who were hired for their brawn rather than their brain. It is harder for today's businesses to disguise from their employees what they are up to or any hidden agenda.

In the new excitement to declare their ethical credentials, companies have sometimes ignored the risks involved. For instance, it is not easy to read the market for ethical goods. Consumers often profess a desire to behave ethically beyond what they are pre-pared to do in practice: 90% of Britons say they oppose caged egg production, yet only 50% of them buy free-range eggs. Many stop buying organic vegetables when they discover how quickly they rot.

Moreover, schadenfreude is as prevalent in the business world as in any other, and those who set them-selves up as ethical role models are easy targets when they fail to live up to their standards. Body Shop's history has been spattered with attempts to discredit its ethical stance, while Starbucks (consistently voted one of America's most ethical firms) has been engaged in a heated and lengthy legal battle over its unauthorised use of the brand names of Ethiopian coffee (see Chapter 1). No doubt when Jesus rose from the dead somebody asked, 'What took you so long?'

BP's fall from grace has perhaps been the most

dramatic in recent years. Having declared that the letters 'BP' stood for 'Beyond Petroleum', the British oil giant tried to move away from its dependence on dirty oil and gas towards clean, renewable forms of energy. But then a series of dreadful (and probably avoidable) accidents in North America took a big bite out of the company's profits and led its hitherto highly acclaimed chief executive, Lord Browne, to fall on his sword and take early retirement in 2007. In the general public's mind in America, BP has changed in a very short space of time from being admired as the cleanest thing in the oil industry to being among the most reviled.

Corporate ethical standards can easily slip because there is no regulator who gives out or withdraws licences to operate based on good behaviour. The setting of standards and the policing of them is an internal affair. If there is a watchdog for ethics it is the whistleblower, the ethical individual whose moral code includes exposing his or her (more frequently 'her') employer's legal and moral wrongdoing to a wider public. But society is still strangely ambivalent towards the whistleblower. While on the one hand being extolled in movies such as *Silkwood* and *Erin Brockovich*, whistle-blowers in practice find it extremely difficult to get another job once they have blown the whistle somewhere.

Most whistleblowers (including some who have helped expose huge scandals inside major corporations) say that they would never, ever do it again. Few end their careers in well-rewarded glory. Most are forced into early retirement where they foster long-standing resentment, and many commit suicide.

If companies are serious about wanting to be more ethical, then they should, first and foremost, ensure proper protection for whistleblowers. And that must include promoting a corporate culture that admires such people in the workplace as much as it does in the cinema. For years, BP tried to ostracise a small number of whistleblowers who worked for the company in Alaska and were warning about the rusting pipelines that criss-crossed the frozen American state. Eventually, the pipelines leaked the equivalent of more than 200,000 barrels of oil into the pristine Alaskan snow, and BP had to pay a heavy price for its high-handed behaviour.

In addition, if companies want to maintain high ethical standards it is important that they pay attention to even the smallest malfeasance. Lynn Brewer, a whistleblower in the Enron case, says that lying and cheating are a state of mind. If it appears in small things it's probably in the big things as well. 'If you spot anything smelly,' she advises young job-hunters, 'run a mile.' Cheating is hideously infectious. Most cheats join in when they see others cheating. One survey found that 56% of American MBA students (the highly competitive corps of top-tier managers of the future) admitted to cheating – usually because they said they knew that others were.

In one significant respect, the movies' whistle-blowers reflect reality – there are many more women than there are men. Women seem less inclined than men to shed their moral persona the moment they pass through their employer's doors. It is no coincidence that it has been businesswomen such as Anita Roddick, Penny Newman, the chief executive of Fairtrade pioneer Cafédirect, and Linda Kaplan Thaler, author of *The Power of Nice* and a founder of one of the fastest-growing advertising agencies in America, who have taken the lead in building ethical businesses. There is probably a thesis to be written on the correlation between ethical business and the presence of women in corporate life. Its conclusion would have to be that there is still too little of both.

At the heart of ethical business, however, there lies a dilemma. For it is, at the end of the day, still business. The Fairtrade movement is determined to sell more and more products – growth and innovation are as central to it as they are to Goldman Sachs and Microsoft. Yet the truly ethical thing to do may be to stop consuming altogether – to say 'No' to a new car every three years, or to yet another electronic gadget, or to another out-of-season strawberry. But that would mean slowing down economic growth itself – and we need to be wary of doing that. For it is only because we are so rich, as western consumers, that we can afford to make moral choices in our shopping, to pay a premium and with it buy a 'feel-good' moment. The African housewife struggling to make ends meet in a Kinshasa market does not have that luxury.

In this book, we'll see how business owners on the front line attempt to marry up the seemingly conflicting pressures on them to work in a way that satisfies their business aims.

1
CREATING AN ETHICAL STRATEGY FOR YOUR BUSINESS

Nick Kettles

Some business owners might be forgiven for thinking that having an ethical strategy represents a compromise with their competitive advantage. But in a world where corporate accounting scandals are prompting legislators and business leaders to embrace the 'triple bottom line' of people, planet and profits, the truth increasingly is that nice guys don't always finish last.

According to the Institute of Business Ethics (IBE), 'Business ethics relate to how any company conducts its business in order to make a profit, while an ethical business, on the other hand, has a much broader agenda and focuses on making a positive contribution to the community'. This is an important distinction. Obviously, it's possible to tick the boxes to show your support for the environment, say, without meeting the same high standards in every other area of your business. Conversely, there may be companies that treat their staff and customers with the utmost honesty, but waste energy and use less-than-ethical suppliers.

In an ideal world, business ethics will inspire ethical businesses. Indeed, the IBE further states that 'A company simply cannot be responsible without also being ethical; a company's core values and codes of ethical behaviour should underpin everything it does'. You have to be willing to 'walk your talk', in other words.

This doesn't mean, however, that ethical trading and profitability are mutually exclusive. Evidence is growing that, as consumers become more globally aware and demand more honesty and transparency, it pays to be ethical. The Co-operative Bank has publicly claimed more than once, for example, that 'Ethical and ecological positioning makes a sizeable contribution to the bank's profitability'.[1]

[1] The Co-operative Bank Partnership Report, 2002.

This can be the case for small businesses, too, and it's not just about reaping the financial benefits of minimising waste, which the Environment Agency says can represent up to 4–5% of turnover, or in manufacturing, up to £1,000 per employee.[2] Shel Horowitz, author of *Principled Profit: Marketing That Puts People First*, believes that, in fact, formulating an ethical strategy can be *the* starting point for creating a more successful business. Horowitz says: 'Business ethics is about applying the common sense of serving the customer and benefiting from the circle of virtue that creates, while also setting the moral parameters of what you are and are not prepared to do.'

Quite. Creating an ethical strategy for your business means a lot more than jumping on the bandwagon and exploiting another niche market. The viral effect of the Internet, which enables consumers to spread ideas and opinions quickly via e-mail and blogs, shines a strong light on the sincere and insincere alike. For example, when Starbucks, who had claimed that they were committed to purchasing their coffee in an ethical and sustainable manner, were found by Oxfam to have tried to block Ethiopian farmers' attempts to file trademark

---

[2] http://www.netregs.gov.uk/netregs/275207/275515/1680156/?lang=_e

applications for its most famous coffee names – denying them potential earnings of up to £47 million annually in the process – the world soon knew about it.[3]

So where to begin?

There's no doubt that a strategy should be thorough, covering every facet of your business, but the simpler it is to formulate, the easier it will be to implement and adhere to. By focusing on three simple steps, the first two of which will be a guiding light for the third, any small business (even sole traders) will be able quickly to formulate a solid ethical strategy to guide and inspire them as well as to create growth.

1. Make your personal principles clear

These personal principles are integral not only in guiding you about what your business is prepared do (and what it isn't), but also in creating the kind of satisfaction levels that will make your customers loyal ambassadors for your product or service.

But don't make this too hard for yourself: you're not trying for sainthood, but you do need to be clear about your values and priorities before you can set out your stall. In the simplest terms, a guiding value should be something you're willing to translate into concrete

---

[3] *The Guardian*, Thursday 26 October, 2006.

commitments that you can make to all of your stakeholders.

So how can you pinpoint exactly what these will be? In her report *Priorities, Practice and Ethics in Small Firms*, Dr Laura Spence, reader in business ethics at Brunel University, indicates that actually, many small business owners already feel strong moral obligations towards their employees and aim to support their local communities. But even if this is how you run your business, it's still good to check that's how your stakeholders actually experience you. Soliciting feedback from suppliers and key customers is a great way to test the temperature and see how well your personal motives match up with the way you run your business.

It should be taken as read that you're following any professional code of conduct which your industry body requires you to sign up to, but it's also important to be realistic about how the values and priorities you choose will be received by the market sector in which you operate. It's good, therefore, also to examine emerging trends in your market sector, to see whether there are already other companies — some of which may be your competitors — that are changing the way they do business. If there aren't, your willingness to change may reap great benefits: today's innovator is often tomorrow's market leader. To illustrate, a growing group of independent financial advisers are making a commitment to be absolutely transparent to win back the confidence of investors who became suspicious of financial products as a result of pension scandals and the 2001 stock market crash.

If you are inspired to make long-term sustainability and/or the environment the focus of your ethical strategy, you could consult the magazines *New Consumer* and *The Ecologist* for inspiration. Both carry ads for ethically inspired businesses along with links to their websites, where many have clearly stated their guiding values and priorities.

If you're still struggling to put your finger on your motivating values, try looking at the issue from the other side: what type of customer would be unacceptable to you? Thinking about the problem in this way can provide the contrast you need to highlight what is most important to you.

For one small company, already committed to honesty and integrity, such a situation actually presented itself, and helped them refine their values still further. While quoting for a job representing at least two months' average turnover, they became aware that their potential customer also directly supplied the arms industry, and therefore the conflict in the Middle East. They felt uncomfortable about this, but at the same time were initially reluctant to turn down the opportunity to pitch for so much work. After close discussion between the founding partners and senior employees, however, they realised that the situation represented a watershed moment and an opportunity to formulate a more precise ethical strategy that would guide them in their future decision-making. In identifying the concept of non-violence as a guiding principle for their company, they realised they couldn't proceed with the tender.

If you find any of the above difficult, or are short of time, you may find it helpful to use Shel Horowitz's 'magic triangle' of quality, integrity and honesty, which could easily form the basis of almost any ethical strategy:

- **quality.** Provide the best value you can.
- **integrity.** Run your business in alignment with your core values; don't try to be something you're not.
- **honesty.** Value the truth and be eager to share it with prospective and existing customers, even if you believe that what they think they want is not actually good for them.

2. Decide what you *are* prepared to do . . . and what you're not

The first step here is to make your values crystal clear in terms of commitments you are willing to make to all of your stakeholders. This is what the IBE calls a code of ethics. One way you may wish to do this is by making a set of statements for each of your stakeholder groups and for each of the values you have chosen. So, using 'integrity' as an example, these statements might look something like this:

- **employees.** We commit always to keep you informed about the financial health of the company.
- **customers.** We will never make statements about our product or service which we cannot substantiate.
- **suppliers.** We will only commit to credit terms we know we can keep.

Obviously these examples are very broad, and you will want to make them specific to your industry, but it is important to keep them simple. Try to express only one idea in each statement, by making it singular, literal and specific. If you find this difficult then simplifying the process in terms of 'will do' and 'won't do' may help.

When it comes to customers you won't work with,

beware of stating the obvious. For example, we can take it for granted that a committed organic farm will not use a chemical fertiliser company as a supplier. But by the same token, it can also be pragmatic to state under which circumstances you *might be* willing to work with those companies that you otherwise wouldn't touch with a bargepole. For instance, one marketing company has stated in its ethical policy that it is prepared to work with companies from traditional industries such as oil and tobacco *if* that work is directly related to long-term sustainability.

3. Make a plan of action

The next step is to formulate a plan of action and actually implement your code of ethics. Unless your business is a new one and developing an ethical product or service from scratch, any plan of action should begin with a thorough examination of your existing offering.

If you have been thorough in steps one or two, you may already have identified whether your product or service does indeed align with your chosen values, especially if you have asked for feedback from your customers and suppliers. If you didn't take that step, now would be a great time to do so: a litmus test of this type can save you a lot of time and money, especially in terms of marketing.

So what do you do if you discover that you need to completely redesign your product or service? If you find yourself facing this situation, then obviously a phased transition to a new offering is sensible, while you take the time to undertake further market research and find new suppliers who do understand and can work within your value system. However, be aware that a balance needs to be struck between your desire to move forward and giving your suppliers a chance to follow you. Take the time to talk to them about what you are going to do, and ask them if they would be willing to provide you with what you want.

No less important is the need to train your staff in how to implement your new code of ethics. Dedicate some time to raising their awareness of the issue involved, through field trips or a presentation. Then follow up with further information in the form of simple guidelines they can follow on a day-to-day basis to implement the company's code of ethics.

It's not uncommon today for companies to state their ethical aims and objectives clearly on their websites, and when it comes to marketing, it's good to make your new ethical aims and objectives crystal clear in all your business communications. But it's also worth considering how your new code of ethics can make the marketing of your product or service both more efficient and more successful. For example, if you have identified the customers you *don't* want to work with, you can focus on communicating with only those that you *do* want to work with. With the proliferation of digital communication channels, more targeted, niche marketing is now both preferred and possible. There are many reputable direct marketing agencies that will be able to sell you so-called 'opt-in' lists of people or businesses who have given their permission to be contacted about certain types of product and service.

Finally, but no less important, you need to make a thorough examination of all the laws you are legally obliged to comply with in your industry, such as the Waste Electrical and Electronic Equipment (WEEE) directive on the safe disposal of electronic goods. You could also consult the environment section of www.smallbusiness.co.uk or the government-funded Envirowise programme (for more information, see Chapters 5 and 8).

Once you have done this, you can decide how far you are willing to go beyond your legal obligations. For example:

■ Do you want to re-source office furniture and canteen refreshment from Fairtrade suppliers?

- What about signing up with a green electricity supplier?
- Why not dispense with a centralised office altogether and enable homeworking?
- How well are you willing to treat your employees? Are they worthy of a profit share?
- What kind of contribution will you make to your local community, as well as to global causes?

For a more detailed discussion of these key issues, turn to Chapter 8.

Applying a plan of action, as suggested on page 19, will provide you with an opportunity to see how watertight your code of ethics is in guiding your business on a day-to-day basis. As your company grows, you may find that you need to refine both your values and the code that expresses them – this will especially be the case if you find yourself facing a particularly tough decision that is difficult to resolve because of a conflict of interests (see Chapter 7). If you are faced with such a dilemma, it's important to give it due consideration through discussion with your business partners and senior employees, and where possible seek third-party advice. The IBE suggests applying a simple test in such situations:

- **transparency.** Do I mind others knowing what I have decided?
- **effect.** Who does my decision affect or hurt?
- **fairness.** Would my decision be considered fair by those affected?

The likelihood is that, as the environmental initiative grows and consumers increasingly demand goods and services that actually deliver on the promise of their advertising, it will be impossible for a business *not* to have an ethical strategy. By adopting one now, you can play your part in raising awareness amongst your employees, customers and competitors while also benefiting from the net savings and job satisfaction that come from facing up to your social and environmental responsibilities as a business owner.

2 FIND SUPPLIERS WHO SHARE YOUR AIMS

Carry Somers

> An ethical business needs to find suppliers who show a respect for both people and planet, fusing social conscience with sustainable development. This chapter will help you to work out your priorities when looking for suppliers who share your aims and will help your business reach its goals.

The first step in this process is to identify the core values that will provide the foundation on which you'll build your ethical purchasing policy. You'll then be able to select and assess your ethical purchasing criteria, and this, in turn, will give you a standard against which to measure suppliers for your particular business. This procedure is intended to place a strong value system at the heart of your decision-making process. As you consciously choose (or remind yourself of) the values on which your business is based, you'll be able to make a positive, informed choice about your suppliers.

Think about core supplier values

Now's the time to think about the values you'll be expecting any supplier you work with to hold. These values are fundamental and non-negotiable. They will be key tenets for your business too, and will transcend any new developments, product cycles or changes in the market or environment.

Make a list of which core values you want your suppliers to have. For example, these might include:

- workers being paid a living wage
- safe and healthy working conditions
- equality in the workplace – no discrimination being practised
- freedom of association – the right to join a union
- no child labour
- no forced labour
- no harsh treatment
- respect for the environment and sustainability of raw materials

Add in any other elements that are particularly pertinent to the industry your business operates in. For instance, if you are setting up an ethical beauty business, your core supplier values will probably include no products being tested on animals.

Fairtrade

If you are setting up a Fairtrade business, you must adhere to a stricter set of criteria known as FINE: visit www.bafts.org.uk/about_criteria_FINE.asp for more information. Also see the IFAT Code of Practice at www.ifat.org: IFAT is a global network of Fair Trade organisations.

If you're not sure where to start when you're thinking about core supplier values, don't worry: there are sources of information to help you get started. For example, take a look at:

- the United Nations Declaration of Human Rights (1948) – www.un.org/Overview/rights.html
- Social Accountability 8000 (SA8000)

standards on labour practices (see www.sa-
intl.org)
- the ETI Base Code, formulated by the Ethical
Trading Initiative (an alliance of trade unions,
non-governmental institutions and businesses
that aims to improve corporate codes of
practice in terms of working conditions). To
find out more, visit www.ethicaltrade.org

Choose the criteria that will create your ethical purchasing policy

Beyond the core supplier values that form the foundation of your ethical business, you will also have many
more key values which apply to your particular business
and the market within which it operates. It is these
values that will help you to build a business with integrity which fits into the value system of both your business and your customers. Your ethical purchasing policy
may change over time with new developments in the
marketplace, but as long as you remain guided by your
core supplier values, it's fine to reassess this policy from
time to time.

Your ethical purchasing policy will set your business apart from the competition and can form the basis of your future marketing and PR strategy. That said, you must make sure that your standards are genuinely adhered to; customers will be extremely wary of companies which start to source ethical products purely to enhance their image or to counteract negative PR.

Next, choose the ethical purchasing criteria you require from a supplier. To help with ideas, you might find it helpful to use the mantra of:

- eliminate
- reduce
- reuse
- recycle
- dispose

(See Chapter 5 for more information on how you can apply 'reduce, reuse and recycle' in your business.)

Below are some ideas to give you a springboard for choosing your own ethical purchasing criteria, grouped under the headings of sustainable, organic, local, ethical and Fair Trade.

Striving for sustainability

Make sure that, wherever possible, you choose suppliers that can give you or promise:

- environmentally sustainable services, such as electricity from renewable sources
- production processes using reduced water/energy/chemicals/non-renewables
- less waste

For example, of the beech-wood pulp used to produce fibres at Lenzing Modal in Austria, 40% produces fibre for environmentally friendly textiles, 10% is a byproduct used to make mints and the rest is used for power generation for the entire plant.

Aim to select products which are:

- recycled
- recyclable
- made from reclaimed materials
- biodegradable and not derived from oil
- from renewable resources, preferably short-life-cycle renewables

- using a minimum of virgin and non-renewable materials
- minimal/recycled/recyclable packaging
- energy-efficient

Organic

- Aim to use organic products certified as such by the Soil Association (www.soilassociation. org.uk) or other reputable bodies. For more information, visit: www.defra.gov.uk/farm/ organic

Local

- Using local suppliers means that as few miles as possible separate you from your supplier. Not only will this cut down on transport and delivery costs, it will help reduce pollution from road traffic and also make sure that the money you spend with them remains in the local economy. The pioneering carbon-neutral eco-community BedZed in London sourced the majority of materials from within 18 miles of the site.
- Look for local co-operative or community organisations with which to collaborate.

- Similarly, are there any local organisations which put a percentage of profits back into the local community?

Ethical

The supplier should:

- adhere to the SA8000 standards mentioned above
- be a member of the Ethical Trading Initiative or another body such as the Ethical Fashion Forum

Fairtrade

The Fairtrade mark is currently only available to certify that raw materials (coffee, sugar and cotton, say) have been subject to independent auditing against a set of Fairtrade criteria. It mainly covers agricultural products and does not cover any handicraft items. Other Fairtrade importers, such as retailers of craft and clothing, can be found through the British Association for Fair Trade Shops (BAFTS; visit online at www.bafts.org.uk) and IFAT and should adhere to the FINE criteria for Fairtrade standards mentioned on page 26.

It is important to remember that if you are hoping to join an ethical organisation, there may be certain minimum standards. For instance, BAFTS stipulates that a majority of products must be purchased from recognised Fairtrade suppliers.

For more ideas, look at the websites of those companies that are known to have a strong ethical policy, such as the Co-operative Bank (www.co-operativebank.co.uk). See Chapter 9 for more advice.

Think about how your products or services relate to your ethical purchasing criteria

Decide which of the criteria above are relevant to your business and write them down on a sheet of paper. Under each of the criteria you have listed, make a note of the products or services which relate to it. (Don't worry if an item falls into more than one category.)

For example, let's say you run a B&B or holiday let, and your aim is to make the premises as sustainable as possible. You decide that the key elements in your ethical purchasing policy are:

- sustainable
- organic
- local
- Fairtrade

Make comments beneath each heading that show how you can marry up what the business does with these elements. For instance:

Sustainable	Organic	Local	Fair Trade
gas and electricity sourced from a green energy supplier using mainly renewable resources	all bed linen and towels to be organic cotton	organic veg box from local farm available for guests	all tea, coffee and sugar provided for guests to carry the Fairtrade mark
furniture made from reclaimed timber		refill environmentally friendly cleaning products at local health food shop	

Write your ethical purchasing policy

Now think about the criteria above and try to place them in order of importance for your business. In this way, if you are fortunate enough to have a choice of ethical suppliers for a product or service, you can find the one which best meets your criteria.

For some businesses, using local suppliers may be the principal way in which they want to make their business more ethical, in that they're reducing the miles which their product has to travel between the supplier and your premises. Others may see Fairtrade as the most important element in an ethical business, as it ensures that producers in the Third World have received fair payment for their work. On the other hand, it may mean that the product has travelled long distances to reach you.

This is quite a conundrum. If you are setting up an organic restaurant, say, your first ethical purchasing criterion for finding a supplier will be, of course, 'organic'. You'll need to think very carefully about the order of subsequent criteria, though. Would you prefer to buy Fairtrade organic honey from Central America, in which case 'Fairtrade' should come high up on the list, or organic honey from a local beekeeper, in which case 'local' should be your next criterion? Working through this process may take some time, but it is the best way of making sure that you find the most appropriate suppliers *for you*.

Combining both your core values and your ethical purchasing criteria, write an ethical purchasing policy for your business. Keep it visible in your office so that all your team are aware of it, and consult it whenever you are looking for a new supplier or assessing current suppliers.

Research your suppliers

The final step is to research available suppliers and then measure them and their products against the above priorities. If you are unsure about the ethics of any of your suppliers, either request a copy of relevant documentation or send them a basic questionnaire so that you can make sure they're compliant with your ethical criteria.

To help with research, you could use some of the following:

- the Internet. You can check www.gooshing.co.uk for the ethical credentials of thousands of manufacturers.
- buy magazines such as *The Ecologist*, *New Consumer* and *Ethical Consumer* to keep up to date with ethical products and services on the

market. *Ethical Consumer* includes buyer's guides and ethical ratings.
■ research a company's ethical and environmental policies. Many companies now carry out an ethical or environmental audit of their business practices.

Tell customers the story behind your products and their provenance

Your customers are putting their trust in your ethical policies. Let them know that this is valued and be open with them about anything which needs improving within your ethical purchasing policy. Ask them for their thoughts and ideas too: as they aren't as involved as you in the nitty-gritty of everyday business life, their objectivity can be a great help.

When selling an ethical product or service, exceed the expectations of your customers by providing high-quality, long-lasting products accompanied by excellent customer service. This will set you apart from other companies and increase your sales and your profile.

Remember, it is no good having an ethical product that just sits on your shelf. The time has long passed when you could sell an ethical product solely on the basis of its provenance. Good design and perform-ance are key, and if you can combine creativity with sustainability you will certainly have happy customers. For example, Unicorn Design (www.unicorndesign.net), based in County Wicklow in the Irish Republic, is a 'Couture with a Conscience' label. Using only certified organic or eco-dyed fabrics made in fair conditions, Sophie Rieu designs clothing with style, character and substance.

3 PLAY YOUR PART IN AN ETHICAL SUPPLY CHAIN

Carry Somers

Businesses have come under increasing pressure from consumers, the media and investors to improve accountability and transparency throughout the supply chain. In broad terms, a supply chain is the network of manufacturers, wholesalers, distributors and retailers that turn raw materials into finished goods and services and deliver them to customers. Supply chains are increasingly being seen as integrated entities, and closer relationships between the organisations throughout the chain can bring competitive advantage, reduce costs and help to maintain a loyal customer base.

Adding an ethical dimension to this mix may seem daunting, but it's crucial if you are to make sure that every part of your business operates in tandem with your values and goals. Writing an ethical sourcing policy is a great start, but the supply chain won't operate ethically as a matter of course: you'll need to work at it, and its effectiveness will depend on how the policy is implemented and communicated throughout the chain, from suppliers through to the final consumers.

Long-term, transparent and consistent relationships are the key to success. Camelot, the National Lottery provider, is well known for its ethical policy and states: 'We aim to work in partnership with all our key suppliers. We want partnerships based on a commitment to each other's success, a realistic understanding of one another's priorities, and a mutual commitment to operate with fairness and integrity.'

In this chapter, we'll look at how even small businesses can play a key role in the supply chain.

Know your supply chain and your place in it

Start off by working out your place within the supply chain of the products and services you purchase. Map out the supply chain for each one as a flow chart, marking clearly any unknown areas, such as the involvement of outworkers. You can highlight this as a potentially increased risk that you'll need to investigate more closely.

> Bear in mind that many manufactured products will have an extremely complex supply chain, with different components coming from different sources, all of which have had a social or environmental impact as a result of their production. Also remember that your analysis should not stop at the stage when the product arrives at your shop or office! To make sure that the chain is genuinely ethical and sustainable, use and disposal (see below and also Chapter 5) also need to be examined.

The main areas to look at are:

- provenance and composition of raw material
- source of components and their manufacture

- assembly/production of finished product
- purchasing — particularly the involvement of intermediaries
- transportation
- storage
- use
- disposal

Recognise potential problems

Your flow chart will have highlighted areas that represent a potential risk in terms of non-compliance. Look at these more closely, and in particular examine issues such as:

- If your suppliers have an ethical policy, how far down the supply chain does this extend? Does it include sub-contractors?
- Do they employ outworkers/homeworkers/casual workers? If so, what rights do they have?
- How many intermediaries are involved in the supply chain? Are they paying a fair price to the people below them in the supply chain? For instance, panama hats can go through as many as seven middlemen who are known as *perros* (dogs) in Ecuador because of their purchasing practices.

- Do your suppliers comply with minimum wages for all workers, irrespective of their status?
- Do they comply with current national, European and international social and environmental legislation? Are they in a position to comply with future legislation? (This is particularly important in the case of harmful chemicals used in the production process, as alternatives need to be sourced *prior* to any ban, to ensure continuation of supply.)
- Be aware of unintended consequences of the implementation of ethical standards, such as double book-keeping.

One potential problem is that, by publicising yourself as an ethical business, you run the risk of attracting unwelcome press coverage if it is found that your supply chain is not complying with its ethical and social responsibilities. Consumers are increasingly aware of these issues through the work of campaigning groups such as Labour Behind the Label (www.labourbehindthelabel.org), which aims to defend the rights of garment workers around the world.

It's not acceptable to use the excuse that you have 'no control' over outworkers or sub-contractors who are making your products, whatever the size of your business: major brands such as Nike and Gap have had to address problems in this area after being affected by consumer boycotts and negative press.

Implement your ethical purchasing policy

If you are starting a new business, you will be looking for suppliers that already adhere to your core supplier values (see page 25) and to as many elements as possible from your ethical purchasing policy (see page 27). Obviously, you will need to make sure your core supplier values are adhered to strictly, as these are non-negotiable. If, however, you've already established your business and have contracts with current suppliers that don't satisfy some or all of the ethical purchasing criteria you've established, you'll need to encourage sustained improvement and to set targets for compliance.

It's crucial that you explain to your suppliers how adhering to ethical criteria will benefit their business: not only is there an increasing demand for suppliers to have an ethical policy, but national, European and international legislation is continually working towards improving labour laws and environmental standards. The UK government has already signed up to the Kyoto Protocol on climate change and Agenda 21 on sustainable development. As a result, your suppliers will benefit in the long term if they improve the social and environmental impact of their supply chain. Educating your suppliers about the importance of maintaining an ethical supply chain, including any forthcoming legislation which directly impacts on your field, is a great way of ensuring future compliance.

Changes can take a long time to implement and so ethical purchasing has to be seen as part of a process of continuous improvement. If you impose high ethical standards too rapidly, suppliers won't have time to comply and both your businesses are likely to suffer. Instead, see the creation of an ethical supply chain as a process of steady, sustained improvement that is fuelled by encouragement and education from your business. For example, one way of making sure that your suppliers are constantly improving the ethical status of their supply chain is to monitor their progress by encouraging them to undertake an ethical audit. This will involve setting targets for improvement in the supply chain, particularly where there are potentially problematic areas in the flow chart you have created for each product.

Be creative in the ways in which you encourage your suppliers to improve their standards. For example, you could encourage:

■ **collaborative projects** in which suppliers work with local organisations or local government to bring about appropriate solutions to regional issues. Collaborating with other companies can be beneficial, as the cost and risk are shared. The construction services group Carillion state in their ethical policy that they are committed to 'Two-way dialogue with all who have an interest in our business, including staff, suppliers, customers, investors, shareholders, appropriate authorities, local communities and other organisations, to identify key environmental issues and to seek innovative solutions and appropriate alternatives'.

■ **stakeholder partnerships**, which can be valuable in building a sustainable supply chain.

■ creating **joint improvement targets** where you work with your suppliers. For instance, you could introduce reusable packaging which can be returned to the supplier.

Another opportunity for a creative approach is within the design process itself. Obviously, the best way to minimise the impact of the life-cycle of a product is to design with sustainability and bio-degradability in mind. If you are having products created specially for your business, encourage suppliers to address issues such as durability, energy use and waste when you brief them.

Communicate your ethical purchasing policy to staff

To give it the best chance of succeeding, your ethical purchasing policy will need to be communicated to anybody within your business who has responsibility for purchasing. It's good practice to draw up a code of conduct which outlines how you expect your ethical purchasing policy to be carried out, so that everyone is clear about parameters.

Purchasing policies do, of course, vary widely between businesses, but they should all include basic elements such as:

- staff training to increase awareness of relevant social and environmental issues. This will also underline the importance of an ethical purchasing policy to the future success of your business.
- making sure staff know who to contact when they have a query or problem
- paying suppliers' bills on time
- looking at the delivery schedules in order to reduce the environmental consequences of transportation
- making sure that small suppliers aren't placed at a disadvantage
- trying not to place more than 20% of your business with one supplier so that they don't become dependent on your organisation for their survival.
- encouraging consideration of 'whole life' costs when assessing purchases. A good example is the difference between buying two sets of rechargeable batteries, plus the cost of a charger, compared to the cost and

environmental impact of buying hundreds of disposable batteries.

Extend the ethical supply chain to include your customers

As a sustainable business, it's essential that you take all available opportunities to show customers how they can:

- purchase responsibly in the first place
- care for their products to ensure maximum longevity
- dispose of the product at the end of its life

The same applies to services. Many utility companies are now educating their customers about how to conserve energy and use less water in such a way that consumption is more responsible.

For some products, such as textiles and electrical goods, the highest environmental impact will occur during their use, so you need to get in early to tell buyers how best to limit this. For example, if you run a clothing company, you could include a care leaflet with every garment that suggests:

- washing at 30 degrees preferably, but 40 degrees max

■ line drying rather than tumble drying

You could also include spare thread and buttons to encourage repairs and thus extend the life of the garment.

Consumers are becoming increasingly aware of issues regarding landfill and are keen to recycle paper, glass and plastics. If the product you are selling does not fall into these categories, it is important to educate your customers about how to dispose of a product at the end of its life. For instance, many companies exist which will rebuild old computers. For household objects, encourage customers to make use of websites such as www.freecycle.org (branches of the Freecycle Network exist all over the world) or to donate items to local charities that work with people on low incomes.

In summary
■ Investigate your supply chain and identify areas of potential risk or concern. At every step along the supply chain, try to come up with creative new approaches to deal with problems.
■ Make sure that your business and your suppliers comply with all relevant environmental and social legislation in your

industry. Keep up to date with EU directives which may affect the future purchasing or disposal of your products.

- Set goals and time frames for suppliers to improve, if they need to. Look for innovative ways you can work together for mutual benefit.

- Encourage and educate your suppliers, staff and end users about the part they can play in ensuring a more sustainable future through reducing the social and environmental impact at every stage of the supply chain.

- Remember that suppliers will always be ready to change *so long as* there is a big enough demand. High street stores and supermarkets now stock recycled, Fairtrade and organic products because their customers wanted them. If retailers and consumers start to demand biodegradable packaging or more energy-efficient appliances, suppliers will undoubtedly meet this demand.

- There is a lot of help available, particularly on how to improve the environmental footprint of your business. Envirowise (www.envirowise.gov.uk; see Chapter 5) is a useful starting point.

A truly ethical supply chain is one where every link in the chain sees both social and environmental improvement as a result of that trade. This should be the goal of every business.

4 CONTRIBUTING TO YOUR LOCAL COMMUNITY

Lesley Somers

Running a successful business using sound ethical principles while at the same time making a contribution to your local community may seem at first glance like too much of a challenge. It is easy to isolate yourself as you make plans and build up your business. It is also easy to imagine that planning community involvement for your business as part of company policy would only weaken your focus on the more important work of running your business.

Not so, according to Charles Handy, one of the world's leading management gurus, who says: 'The companies that survive longest are the ones that work out what they uniquely can give to the world.'[1]

My hope is that at the end of this chapter you will realise that you can't afford *not* to think community-wide when planning your business objectives.

What's in it for you?

Styles of business leadership have changed. We now treat our staff as colleagues who help us reach our company's goals, rather than as workhorses. They bring with them into your business talents and abilities that can enrich everything you do. And they also bring their community connections with them — their partners and families, their friends and interests, their ideals and commitments.

When we view workers in this way, it follows that we'll see reasons and opportunities for interaction with our local community. Some issues may be very close to

---

[1] Handy, Charles. 'The Search for Meaning', *Leader to Leader* 5 (Summer 1997): 14–20. This article is available on the Leader to Leader Institute website at: www.leadertoleader.org/knowledgecenter/L2L/summer97/handy.html

home and involve the 'community' of staff inside the workplace. For example:

- adequate childcare options for employees
- encouraging staff to use public transport, rather than cars, to get to work

But there is also the wider community situated around the premises to consider. We have the option of accepting the opportunities and restrictions of the local communities as we find them, or of being a voice and a positive influence within that community for co-operation, growth, partnerships and change.

But is community involvement worthwhile for you? What's in it for your business? Well, benefits can include:

- boosting goodwill and co-operation locally within the community
- increased access to local community resources
- opportunities for opening new markets, or making new contacts
- a great platform for PR, and positive media coverage
- a committed workforce, and good business relationships

■ a sense of support for your business and ownership of its ideals by a wide range of people

With these benefits, can you afford *not* to be community-orientated? Getting involved will take some careful planning, but will be well worth the effort.

Talk to the people you work with

Once you've decided to take the plunge, have a meeting with your staff – or anyone else closely involved with your business – to talk through the issues and to get their feedback. To make sure you're focused on what your local community needs, ask yourselves:

■ What are people in the local community interested in?
■ What do they see as the local needs?
■ What do they worry about locally?
■ Where are the limitations in the community?
■ Where are the opportunities?
■ What talents and skills do your work colleagues have that could help to spearhead your interaction with the community?

Make a summary of all the ideas and suggestions first of all, without dismissing any of them. Then go back and look at your list in more detail, scrutinising each suggestion more carefully. Don't dismiss any seemingly wacky or crazy ideas out of hand; while they may not work as they stand, *elements* of them might work very effectively. At this stage, strike a balance between being realistic and being innovative. While you're discussing the options on the table, try to reach a consensus together on where your business could appropriately make a contribution to the local community, and become involved.

During this process, issues may come up which aren't appropriate for your business to deal with: you could be concerned about anything from levels of crime to local recycling provisions. If possible, though, someone should follow up this discussion by raising genuine concerns with the appropriate local service providers: talk to the police, your local council or your neighbourhood councillor to flag things up.

Important guidelines to adopt for this part of the process

■ Match your business's products and services to local needs. For example, if your company makes toys, educational equipment or books, it would make sense to get involved with childcare providers in your area.

- From your discussions, choose a specific 'area of interest' and consider imaginative ways in which you can make a contribution.
- Start off small, and plan ways in which you can expand your involvement in the future.
- Set parameters for your involvement, in terms of both time and financial commitment.
- Keep in mind that your staff should enjoy community involvement – you don't want it to become a chore, so plan in some fun as well.

Getting to grips with the reality of involvement

You now need to make things happen. The first task should be to appoint a member of staff to have special responsibility for community affairs. In consultation with this person:

- Set up regular forums where you can discuss community issues with staff.
- Set up regular slots to discuss these with other managers, if your business is big enough.
- Link your PR with actions in the community.

- Integrate your community involvement with the future plans you make for your business.
- Look for people or groups within the local community who have expertise and experience within the field that you are interested in. Ask them in to discuss possibilities for working together and potential partnerships.
- Set up a trial period for involvement – say three months – and evaluate the experience at the end of this period.

Check thoroughly the legislation governing any sector within which you are planning to work. For instance, you will need Criminal Records Bureau (CRB) clearance for your staff if you are planning to work with young people. For more information, visit: www.crb.gov.uk

Don't discount the competition!

Wherever possible, take the viewpoint that other businesses in your community involved in the same area of work as you provide opportunities for co-operation. This is much healthier than viewing them purely as competition, even though this may now be an ingrained habit! Purely in terms of the *community's* needs at this stage, are there any services or knowledge that you offer that could actually complement each other?

And in the longer term . . .

After your trial period, and when the evaluation process has been completed, you will have a good idea of what is necessary for any long-term community involvement. You will be able to assess the strengths and weaknesses of the particular way in which your community project worked, and no doubt you learned some useful lessons along the way. Now is the time to be very honest with yourselves and your staff, and ask yourselves the following:

- Did the experiment work?
- Could we have done better?
- In light of what we have learned, what long-term involvement do we want to opt for?
- What would we do differently next time?

Don't be afraid of having another three-month trial period working in another sector of the community if you feel that you didn't make the best choice in your initial attempt. It will be a trial and error process for many businesses, so don't be too disheartened.

So what comes next?

The wise way forward is to set up a well-thought-through 'community involvement policy' (CIP) for your business, which makes sure that your community involvement is well embedded through every area of your work. As an example, the clothing and footwear retailer Timberland have a useful 'Community Investment Guide' (to find it, go to www.timberland.com and look for their 'Community Involvement' section). Their staff spend time as volunteers involved in local community action to 'lessen their ecological footprint'. This action dovetails nicely with the whole focus of the company's business.

Evaluating the ongoing effect of your work in the community is essential. Many companies are now adopting a form of 'social auditing', a process that enables an organisation to assess its social, economic and environmental benefits and limitations. It is a way of measuring the extent to which that organisation lives up to the shared values and objectives that it committed itself to when it created its CIP. For more information, visit the Social Audit Network (SAN) online at: www.socialauditnetwork.org.uk

Do remember, of course, that having a CIP doesn't exempt you from taking care of your employees in other, more traditional ways. For example, one small business had an excellent community involvement policy, but had forgotten to institute a health and safety policy for its workers. The media had a field day when this became public knowledge.

It's also important for you to strike a balance. In supporting one sector of the community – such as those campaigning on green issues, say – check that you are not alienating another sector of the community. Don't forget to assess the effect of your involvement on every area of community life.

Other ways of interacting with your community

The adage 'think globally, shop locally' can be applied to your business sourcing. Why not map your local area to find out what is available? With some imaginative thinking, you may be able to use local craftsmanship to produce, for instance, unique display materials for your business. Pachacuti (see page 137) sourced many of their shop fittings from a local blacksmith, for example, and the resulting beautiful wrought ironwork adds to a feeling of luxury in the shop. Also, visiting a local reclaimed timber yard, we discovered wood from a dismantled old pier. Using the skills of a local carpenter, this well-worn wood was turned into beautiful shelving and display tables.

Schools

A business set in the community can be a valuable asset for training for school leavers. Discuss with headteachers or the Local Education Authority how you can be involved. Be prepared to offer training and work experience, if appropriate.

There are many opportunities for a business to interact with the community, so be creative. You could think about:

- sponsoring local events or offering prizes for sports days
- helping to resource, and getting involved with,

local celebrations such as carnivals or street parties

- holding an 'open day' when the local people are invited to spend a few hours in your premises so that you can inform them about what you do, involve them in it and (hopefully!) have fun in the process
- partnership with local organisations, for your mutual benefit
- working with national or international service providers, and passing on some of the benefits to your local community
- building a good relationship with your local and regional press offices. Let them know that a representative from your business will be made available to comment on any topical ethical issue. Prepare press releases, and make them available on your website.
- partnership with other local businesses for mutual support, promotion, etc

And the list could go on!

Your business as an example of ethical good practice within the community

If you want to take a lead in encouraging ethical responsibility within your community, you need to make sure that your business operates as an excellent example. People won't listen to you if they can see that you're not following the maxims you're asking others to take on board. Consider issues of waste management, recycling and minimising unnecessary pollution. You may need to share cars, and to take measures like seeking to limit any unnecessary overseas trips.

People will be looking to you to take a lead on ethical issues. They may also criticise harshly any perceived wastage on your part. You will need to be prepared to examine your personal priorities – for example, do you turn up to work in a gas-guzzling car? You also need to be prepared to address any ethical issues or challenges that may come your way. See Chapter 7 for more information on this issue.

Once you consider options of how to get involved with the local community, endless opportunities will present themselves. Your dilemma will be how to choose wisely, and how to make sure that your involvement is well founded, thorough, followed up and evaluated, and that it genuinely does benefit and empower your community.

Keep up to date!

The growth in ethically based businesses is extraordinary at the time of writing. As a committed business-owner or manager, make sure you keep up to speed with the latest developments in ethical practice in your industry, considering the challenges they present and how these relate to your interactions with the local community.

There are now many online sources of help that can support you as you do this, so make a start by looking at:

- Corporate Social Responsibility.gov.uk: www.csr.gov.uk
- Business in the Community: www.bitc.org.uk
- Community Links: www.communitylinks.org

5 CREATING AN ETHICAL WORKPLACE

Carry Somers

Creating an ethical workplace that works in tandem with your business's goals can help you become more competitive and also have a measurably positive effect on your finances. It's now easier than ever to source eco-friendly equipment and services for your business – everything from teabags to an Internet connection – and by reducing your expenses on these items, you'll be freeing up more funds that you can plough back into the business or other causes you support.

The aim of this chapter is to look at the areas of your business that can most benefit from a thorough review and then to draft an achievable action plan that details the actions you will take to improve the ethical impact of your business in those areas.

Review your workplace

To identify areas for potential improvement in your workplace, you'll first need to review current practice and procurement.

Begin by focusing on the following key areas:

- office supplies and equipment
- utilities – particularly electricity and water
- waste and recycling

Depending on the industry your business operates in, there may, of course, be other areas that you need to include from the outset, but those above are the bedrock you can base your assessment on. (You can also add more headings at a later date when you have already achieved some of your initial goals.) At this early stage, though, concentrate on the main purchases which you make on a regular basis. Under the utilities heading, you will need to examine not only the provider of the service, but also how you use that service, as the aim will be to find ways to minimise consumption.

Under the above headings, make a list of *current* business practice. Involve everyone in the business to get their perspective and experience and list everything you can think of. Don't dismiss anything as too small a change to make at this stage or 'not worth it' – at least look into it first! For example, under the 'office supplies and equipment' heading, you might write:

- **Paper.** It's approved by the Forest Stewardship Council (FSC) but not recycled.
- **Printers.** Always left on at night.
- **Drinking cups.** We go through hundreds of plastic cups a week and have no way to recycle them at the moment.

As you and your colleagues start to work through this review, ask yourselves some key questions about what you do and how you do it and then suggest action points. For example:

- **How can we reduce electricity consumption?**

  Action point: make sure that staff turn off equipment at the end of the day. The last person out of the office should check that printers, monitors and lights have not been left on.

■ How can we get the maximum use out of products?

Action point: make sure that paper is printed on both sides before we recycle it.

■ How can we increase the longevity of products we purchase?

Action point: we should buy rechargeable batteries.

■ How can we reuse some of the waste we create?

Action point: we could shred paper that is about to be recycled and use it for packaging. Or make notepads from sheets that have only been used on one side.

Examine your office supplies and equipment

Businesses in the UK use around 5 million tonnes of printing paper every year, with the average office worker using one tree's worth of paper per year. If you keep the mantra of 'reduce, reuse, recycle' in your head, you'll find it easy to think of ways to cut down the amount of office supplies you buy. Here are just a few ideas based on the above:

Print and paper

■ Contrary to the dream of the 'paperless office', paper usage is continuing to grow in UK companies. The easiest way to work out whether your business is printing documents unnecessarily is, of course, to look in the nearest waste paper bin! When you need to print a document, look at the settings for 'margins' and 'page setup' on your computer so that you can get as much text on the page as possible and reduce the number of pages you'll need to print. If everyone in the company does this, you'll soon begin to see a big difference.

If you need to distribute information to your team, you could e-mail it to them or, better still, put it on your intranet site. You'll save on paper and also won't fill up your colleagues' inboxes in the process. If that option isn't available, simply put one copy of the info on a prominent notice-board in your office or factory, and then ask people to look out for it.

- Use the reverse side of paper for printing. Set the photocopier to double-sided printing as its default and use the duplex option on laser printers when printing multiple pages.
- GreenPrint software (http://printgreener.com) is an easy way to eliminate those wasteful pages which are printed out automatically at the end of a document, often containing just an advert or legal information. By analysing all of the pages sent to the printer, it can remove any unnecessary pages before they are printed.
- Office paper is of a very high quality and can be recycled at least five times. For businesses based in London, The Laundry (www.thelaundry.biz) is a weekly kerbside recycling solution which will collect paper, recycle it and sell it back to you. They are also able to recycle computers, CDs and toner cartridges.
- The government-funded programme Envirowise (www.envirowise.gov.uk) will carry out a free environmental audit for you through one of their *Fast*Track visits, provided you fulfil their criteria, and will also offer advice on all aspects of recycling and energy-saving.
- Similarly, the Waste Action Resource

Programme (WRAP) is another government initiative and advice service designed to minimise waste and encourage recycling (www.wrap.org.uk). For more information, visit www.wasteonline.org.uk

- Buy office products that last longer such as heavy duty, preferably recycled, files as this will both reduce waste and save money over time.

- Register with the mail preference service (MPS) to reduce unwanted junk mail (www. mpsonline.org.uk). Ask companies that inundate you with office supplies catalogues to send a full catalogue just once a year and to cancel interim updates. You can always check their websites or ask about special offers when placing an order.

- Sign up to a green, sustainable stationery supplier for everything from padded bags to Post-it notes. Look out for the FSC logo on paper and other wood-based products which come from certified, well-managed forests. Even better, buy recycled paper products.

- If every office worker in the UK used one less staple every day it would save 120 tonnes of steel a year! Change to reusable fasteners such as paperclips or bulldog clips or use staple-less staplers (these hold up to five sheets of paper together by punching holes or tiny strips through them).

Computers

The average computer is replaced every two or three years as a result of advances in technology. As almost 2 tonnes of raw material is required to produce a desktop and monitor, extending the life of a computer by upgrading memory and storage space is essential for an ethical office.

- When purchasing equipment such as computers and printers for your workplace, check the best price available and the ethical rating of the manufacturer at www.gooshing.co.uk, a guide to ethical shopping from the makers of *The Good Shopping Guide*. Look for computers, keyboards and printers that bear the TCO label (TCO Development certifies products that meet both environmental standards *and* ergonomic design criteria).
- To find your nearest computer recycler, visit www.wasteonline.org.uk. The Ethical Computer Centre (TECC) is a project that reuses

73

unwanted computer equipment, which it sells at an affordable price to communities in the UK and in developing countries. For more information, visit: www.teccshop.org.uk

- Consider signing up to an ethical Internet service provider (ISP), such as Green ISP (www.greenisp.co.uk), where your money will be used to support charitable and environmental projects.

- When your inkjet cartridges or laser toners are empty, send them to be recycled or refilled. You can recycle cartridges and help charities at the same time if you recycle with Accutecc (www.accutecc.co.uk), Cartridges4charity (www.cartridges4charity.co.uk) or Oxfam's Laserxchange (www.laserxchange.co.uk) . Purchasing refilled cartridges need not compromise print quality: a *Which?* survey found very little difference between refilled and branded cartridges.

Reduce consumption and look at alternative utility providers

Utilities bills make up a large proportion of a business's overheads, so whether you're operating on a shoestring budget or not, it makes sense to regularly review what you pay. The added ethical context that we're looking at here is no longer as much of a hurdle as it used to be. Thanks to the Internet, it's much easier to research and find out about different options, and the range is growing all the time.

- Envirowise (see above; www.envirowise.gov.uk) can provide free on-site visits to help you to save energy and use your resources more efficiently.
- Remember to switch off all lights, computer equipment and printers at night. Also, make sure that computers are set to shut down monitors after a period of inactivity.
- If you have a retail outlet, don't keep the door open when the heating is on and put window lights on a timer so they are not left on all night.
- Consider switching your electricity to a green energy tariff. You can either switch to a company supplying electricity which is generated from renewable sources or choose a green tariff from a company that supplies an equivalent amount of renewable energy into the national grid. uSwitch (www.uswitch.com) will provide information on the cheapest green tariff in your area.

■ Businesses can write off the whole capital cost
of investment in energy-saving technologies
and machinery in the first year. Find out more
at www.eca.gov.uk

Cut down on waste and set up recycling schemes

When you start your campaign to reduce waste, begin
by looking closely at what gets thrown away and then
look for ways to recycle this waste. What *your* office may
consider waste – cardboard boxes or cellophane bags,
say – could easily be used by another business within
your locality for packaging.

Next, contact your local council to find out about
recycling facilities in your area. In many towns and
cities, there is a regular paper or cardboard collection
service at a nominal charge, but if not, you may need to
take recyclables to the nearest recycling point. Find out
what can and what cannot be recycled, as it does vary
from place to place.

■ You may also need to organise containers for
collecting recycling, and their size will depend
upon the frequency of collection; some
collectors, though, will provide businesses with
special containers for recycling, or even with

skips in the case of cardboard recyclers. Place recycling bins near to office desks, preferably closer than the waste bin!

- Confidential waste will need to be shredded. If you shred on the premises, the recycling will take up more space but you can find collectors who will provide a certificate to guarantee that documents have been destroyed. A quick search on Google or another search engine for firms operating in your area should give you some good leads.

- Encourage staff to use mugs rather than disposable cups for coffee. Alternatively, Save A Cup (www.save-a-cup.co.uk) will provide a cup-stacking bin system which collects polystyrene cups and they will then recycle them.

- Remarkable (www.remarkable.co.uk) converts plastic cups into pencils and also produces a wide range of office stationery from recycled sources, such as mouse mats made from car tyres.

Don't forget to involve the office cleaners! There is little point in separating out material for recycling if it then gets mixed up with the rest of the rubbish.

Think about other ethical improvements

- Providing Fairtrade drinks for staff is an easy improvement to make in any workplace. Consult www.fairtradeatwork.org.uk for information on why businesses have started using Fairtrade products. The website's 'Out of Home Directory' lists UK distributors that are able to supply businesses with Fairtrade products, including drinks for vending machines.

- There is a growing range of ethical banking and insurance options for business in the UK, which we look at in more detail in Chapter 9.

- Encourage staff to car-share, if they have to drive to work. Consider carbon-offsetting your business travel: HM Revenue & Customs (www.hmrc.gov.uk) produce a fact sheet on green travel that is helpful for employers intending to set up a travel plan, while the website www.cyclescheme.co.uk gives information on tax-free bicycles for employees. For walkers, the walkit website (www.walkit.com) suggests routes for the quickest way to walk from A to B. It may not be appropriate for every business (if you operate in a rural area, say, where people may live several miles from where they work), but it's a great way to cut down on car use and boost fitness in the process.

Create an action plan

Now you've worked through the key areas above (and any others specific to your business or industry), it's time to draft an action plan outlining how you will make improvements in each area. Formalising your ideas in this way gives them a greater chance of really happening, and it's also a good way for you to monitor your progress.

Your plan should include the following:

- What actions need to be carried out to make the workplace more ethical?
- How will you achieve the action?
- Who will carry it out?
- How will improvements be measured?
- Who is responsible for monitoring the action plan?

Also, make sure that your plan is realistic and achievable. It's great to aim high, but if you go too far and don't achieve your inflated targets, people will become discouraged.

Keep track of your progress regularly and ask for feedback from members of staff: have they spotted any problems or noticed any potential areas for further improvement? As mentioned above, a noticeboard or bulletin board online can spread the good news and also give your staff a place to make their suggestions.

Be flexible and be ready to change some aspects of your approach if you need to once things are up and running; you can also update your plan to include more ambitious goals if things are going well.

Educating people about the benefits of working like this is a big part of the battle, so keep everyone informed of how you're doing and remember to congratulate them on any milestones you reach and any savings made. That way, everyone will benefit from the 'feel-good' factor of contributing to an ethical workplace.

6
TREATING YOUR STAFF FAIRLY

Lorenza Clifford

Looking after your staff can make a lot of business sense on many levels. Recruiting new employees can cost thousands of pounds, while losing staff who have been with you a while not only means that valuable experience and knowledge are leaking out of the business, but also means that morale could slump. There are plenty of incentives for getting it right, and how you treat your staff should be just as important a part of your business as your commercial values and goals.

Many larger organisations have tuned into this already, and in recent years employee assistance services have sprung up in western workplaces to provide welfare support to staff. Small business owners are often motivated by social considerations as much as by profit, and many feel strong moral obligations towards their employees.

But what does treating your staff ethically *really* entail? The bottom line is that it means understanding the impact that your business decisions can have on the lives of others and acting in such a way that, overall, you have a *positive* impact. In the UK, there are many laws governing the treatment of staff, and complying with that legislation is an important part of the picture. How can you be sure that you are doing well? Below, we consider some of the areas that you may need to think about.

Select on the basis of merit

Selection on the basis of merit means giving the job to the most deserving candidate. The implication is that you want to select applicants who:

- have the ability to perform the job well without suffering undue stress
- are motivated to work well in their position
- will enhance their team

■ will improve the organisation's likelihood of success in the future

There are many good reasons for meritocratic selection. Here are just three of them:

1. The law forbids you to discriminate on the grounds of membership of unions, gender, sexual orientation, age, disability, race, religion or belief.
2. If you focus on merit you will get the best person for the job.
3. It enhances the reputation of your organisation and makes recruiting in the future easier.

You can select people meritocratically and see the benefits by:

■ using a standardised process, evaluating all candidates against the same criteria
■ making sure that the content of interviews / assessments is clearly linked to job content
■ giving the opportunity for potential employees to learn in detail about the role, the workplace,

duties to be performed and expectations you have as an employer
- allowing time to answer applicants' questions honestly and frankly
- considering the selection process itself, to check that it is not abusive (for example, that it doesn't take too long or, if it is lengthy, that sufficient breaks are offered)
- giving enough feedback to rejected applicants (who have invested their time in approaching you), especially if they ask for it, so they can understand and learn from the experience

Be aware of fair employment conditions

Since October 2004, all employers must set out for their staff the dismissal and disciplinary rules and the new minimum statutory procedures in writing. To dismiss an employee fairly, you must first have a fair reason for doing so. The potentially 'fair' reasons include:

- conduct
- retirement
- capability
- redundancy
- a statutory or contractual requirement

Of course, when you are running an ethical business, the requirement in law should be the threshold or bare minimum level of fairness, rather than the ultimate test.

Discourage heat-of-the-moment decisions in favour of a thought-through investigation and process in the cool light of day. Outline a proper process for grievances in advance, rather than waiting until the first problem comes up. If conflict arises, engage in 'good faith' negotiations; in other words, try to come to an amicable arrangement if possible, rather than assuming the worst or acting in a way that might blow up an issue out of proportion.

Employees should feel that they are free to report either a grievance or suspect behaviour without fear of retaliation. On top of the fact that this is only fair, it makes good business sense to sort things out internally before they escalate. You need to know what is happening as early as possible, so if your business has managers (other than you) leading the team, ask them to operate an open-door approach where possible, so that staff feel comfortable raising issues and know they will be heard. Bear in mind that the above only works where the reaction of managers to issues raised is positive and timely. The proper handling of reports of misconduct within the company will demonstrate to your staff that executives are concerned with doing the right thing. If reports of misconduct are ignored or poorly handled, then staff will stop telling you about grievances, and the first you'll hear about problems may be at an industrial tribunal.

Be aware that business decisions you make may have serious employment consequences. If your business cannot pull out of a downturn, or if your industry and market change so much that redundancies cannot be avoided, do what you can to limit the effects when you have to reduce the size of your workforce. For example, be ready to work closely with unions, government agencies, outplacement agencies and other groups. It is not just about *what* you do when you make these big decisions, but *how* you do it.

Action in ethics is worth so much more than any policy. The underlying message throughout this book is 'Do as you would be done by', and for good reason. Though simple, it sums up the message informing ethical business.

Provide a safe working environment

You have a legal responsibility for the health and safety of your employees and anyone else who may be affected by your business. Health and safety law requires you to carry out an assessment of the risks in your workplace. Here is a simple seven-step process to help you:

1. Identify any potential hazards in the working environment.
2. Identify who might be harmed by the hazards and how.
3. Identify precautionary measures already in place.
4. Assess the risk.
5. Record what you have found.
6. Recommend improvements to precautions.
7. Review at regular intervals.

Try to keep it simple but thorough, especially if the environment is not complex. If you are at all unsure about your obligations, the Health and Safety Executive's website is a useful source of help and further information. Visit www.hse.gov.uk or call the Infoline on 0845 345 0055.

Going beyond this, what would make your company a fantastic working environment where employees will gladly come? What can you do about all the aspects of environment in terms of making work a pleasant place to be? Consider the following:

■ **personal and property security.** Think about what you can provide in terms of personal safety awareness, access control, visible crime prevention, eg property marking, premises foot patrols, CCTV, as appropriate, a plan for lone-working situations and off-site working.

- **quality of buildings.** Make sure that all workplaces are in good repair and that there is enough ambient lighting, noise and draught exclusion and fresh air. Ideally, working areas should be laid out ergonomically.

- **interior decoration.** Your staff should have good surfaces, up-to-date decor, plants and artwork where appropriate, good lighting, and comfortable ergonomic furniture.

- **cleanliness.** Work surfaces should be appropriately cleaned, windows, walls and floors regularly attended to, washroom supplies regularly replenished, and eating and food preparation areas should be spotless.

Provide adequate rest and time off

Working hours, holiday and rest time are governed in the UK by working time regulations. There are circum-stances under which businesses may be exempt or can request employees to opt out.

Before you consider exemptions, bear in mind that these regulations were drawn up to reduce health and safety incidents related to exhaustion and stress-related illnesses linked with long-term overwork. In an ethically run business, the best interests of staff are put along-side other business interests. In the long run, you may find your business more profitable and better regarded if you introduce employment practices that help employees achieve a better work–life balance. Remem-ber, all employees are entitled to a good work–life balance, not just those with caring responsibilities. Enabling employees to feel more in control of their working life can lead to increased productivity, lower absenteeism and a happier, less stressed workforce.

Do you have a healthy attitude to rest and recuper-ation? We all need rest and relaxation to maintain a happy and productive mindset, and you probably recog-nise that this is true logically. But what are your under-lying beliefs about time off? When you rest, do you have a little voice telling you that you're lazy? When others rest, do you think they are shirking?

Think about the cultural aspects of your staff taking the time that you already allow: do people feel that because their boss works late, they should too? Setting a good example with your own work–life balance is a great way to proceed. Then encourage others to follow suit. If your staff are motivated, you will soon see the benefits.

Pay properly for the job

Make sure you are paying decent wages. There are, of course, laws covering the minimum wage, but these are only a starting point. It is a false economy to underpay: if your employees are struggling to make ends meet, their minds will not be on the job, which can lead to problems with the quality of their work or even health and safety issues.

Not paying enough is a clear demotivator, but what about payment at the other end of the spectrum? Do top wages produce higher motivation? The Institute of Work Psychology suggest that they are a general reinforcer, since people can choose to use pay for whatever they like. But it seems that performance-related pay often fails to transform performance in the way that was intended. If you plan to introduce a performance-related scheme, it is really important to assess people's performance fully and accurately, so that it is strongly linked with rewards. Any perception of unfairness would reduce the effectiveness of the change you are trying to make.

Pay men and women equally for work of equal value. Many employers, including the government, are lagging behind the legislation in this area, but your employees have the right to ask you for information to help them work out whether you are paying them equally.

Remember that you are not entitled to employee motivation and loyalty just because you are paying people for their services. You must earn these, by genuinely valuing your employees. If you want to create a culture where people help each other, look out for each other's well-being and truly want to see one another succeed, then encouraging gratitude in your managers is critical – it's motivational rocket fuel!

Provide good-quality training

The importance of training should be reinforced from your staff's first day with you: induct them properly, giving them a good introduction to the workplace, the work and the people they'll have most frequent contact with. This will reduce stress and make sure that your new staff member can be productive and safe from day one. It also shows that you value them, which is the right motivational message to give from the kick-off.

Having a clear, concise, easily applied ethics and values statement ensures that your expectations are clear and may reduce the number of situations that need to be referred upwards. Encourage employees to develop relevant and transferable skills and assist them by providing any training and coaching they need to do a good job. As long as training is relevant to the activities of the job and attention is paid to the transfer of learning into the workplace, you should see the results of development activities in the bottom-line results.

For example, consider carefully before you decide which skills are priorities for your staff; the answer might not be as obvious as you at first think. Dig about with some questions to find out what would make the biggest difference to them. For instance, the area of communication breaks down into many skill sets: written work, presentations, listening skills, engaging in conversation, and so on. Which are most important? Concentrate on just one or two at a time, then follow up training by asking staff what they learned and what they are going to do differently in their work as a result. Ask what you can do to help them apply their learning and what support they need from others. This will maximise the return on your investment in the training and can enhance employees' motivation and loyalty. It will also improve your reputation as an employer, making it easier to recruit in the future.

It is said that employees don't leave companies, they leave managers. So, the managers in your business need proper training to ensure that they know how to manage people as well as how to manage projects and information. You need them to do the best for your business through the way that they lead.

Coaching can add a dimension of support to the

development of managers and leaders. It offers the space to do thinking work and can be a catalyst to take different perspectives on difficult problems and tricky situations. In addition, a coach can offer feedback on soft skills that help individuals to improve. Benefits typically reported by those who have been coached are reduced stress, increased self-awareness and effectiveness, and better decision-making. While coaching is something that a business *can* operate without, a really good coach can easily make a good return on the investment you put in through these benefits, and may make all the difference in helping you differentiate your company from the competition. Some coaching companies even offer a guarantee on the results of their coaching.

Involve your staff in decisions that affect them

You need to have proper two-way communication channels that are open at all times. In times of change, making sure that your staff are kept in the loop consistently will be a key way of taking them along with you. People tend to be naturally resistant to change, so you'll need to go the extra mile to combat this tendency and to get employees to see it in a positive light.

To start off on the right foot, ask staff for feedback

and suggestions when change projects initially get going. Keep up the momentum as the projects proceed, and meet with managers and employees regularly to explain the decisions you have made, the reasons for any changes, how they will be enacted and what effect they will have on them. You can also ask people what (if any) rumours they may have heard – and then tackle any unfounded ones head-on. This approach is especially useful in times of stress and uncertainty – if your business is taking over another, for example, or if yours is the subject of another company's interest.

You may be aware of the ICE regulations (Information and Consultation of Employees) 2005. As of April 2008, these regulations affect all businesses with 50 or more employees. They give employees the right to be kept in the picture about issues affecting their employment, or the way their work is organised. While talking to people face to face is often the best way to get your point across, sometimes it's just not possible: your business may operate in shifts, say, or it may be growing quickly. There are still many ways you can get a message to your staff, though, even if you can't all get together at the same time, so think about using:

- e-mail
- the company intranet

■ a noticeboard
■ newsletters

The DirectGov site has a useful summary of the ICE regulations at: www.direct.gov.uk/en/Employment/ Employees/ResolvingWorkplaceDisputes/DG_ 10028095

Finally, make sure you think about *the order in which you communicate things* to people. A cautionary tale: canteen staff for a large organisation were surprised one day by the kind commiserations of their customers, who had heard by e-mail that the canteen was to close! This is *not* the way to treat your staff.

7 TACKLING AN ETHICAL BUSINESS CONUNDRUM

Lorenza Clifford

Managing an organisation ethically makes sound business sense for many people. Making a profit need not involve being part of a chain in which someone is being exploited along the way; it can come from participating in sustainable, supportive, contributory business activities. Reading this book, you will already have realised that there are many ways to offer your customers the products and services they want, while bringing benefits to people and the environment along the way.

But there may be times when a potentially lucrative business proposition comes along that would, at first glance, seem to contradict your ethical standards. Or something in your current mode of operations may come to light that conflicts with your ethical business principles. How can you turn this into a positive opportunity for your business?

Looking at the issue in context

Ethical businesses have an added layer of complexity to the context within which they must operate. Not only do they have to make decisions that work commercially, but they also need to operate within a set of strict criteria that define their goals and practices. As with other pioneers, the paths are not necessarily well marked out by those who have gone before – there are no paths in some cases. However, looking at some key points will help you break down the issue facing you into more manageable sections.

Customer perceptions

Consumer power has been mobilised towards ethical businesses for some time. The risk of marketing ethical credentials is that, should you be perceived to underperform, you may be charged with hypocrisy and deserted by your customers in droves.

The Body Shop is an excellent example of both these points: the first shop was opened over 30 years ago in Brighton, and was a standard-bearer for Anita Roddick's commitment to her principles of ethically sourcing ingredients until 2006, when the chain was bought by the giant French conglomerate L'Oréal. While Dame Anita felt that L'Oréal was open to learning from the Body Shop's stances on issues such as community trading, many customers felt betrayed and disappointed by the move.

Similarly, Google, founded in 1998, has always been very clear about its corporate policy ('do no evil': see www.google.com/corporate/tenthings.html), but a series of controversial initiatives, such as its decision to remove references that the Chinese government would object to when it launched its Chinese-language version, rocked public opinion. While the company fought back by claiming that it was better that it provided some information to Chinese users than none at all, many remained unconvinced.

While your business won't be as big or command as much world-wide attention (or at least, not yet!), you could still feel a backlash if customers feel you've let them down.

Meaning

Does your workforce buy in to your ethical stance? Your people may not care as profoundly about the issues as you do – which could leave you acting as 'big brother' in your own organisation. On the other hand, if your people are signing up for the same issues as you are, part of your employees' motivation may come from working for an ethical employer. That being the case, it could help reduce your turnover and increase the ease with which you can recruit.

Existing and future legislation

Environmental laws are already one part of your business that you cannot afford to ignore. The Environment Agency (www.environment-agency.gov.uk) prosecutes around 700 businesses each year for failure to comply with legislation. And claiming that you're not aware of a law is no excuse: it's your responsibility to be up to speed with the requirements relevant to your industry. If you're running along sustainable principles, you should be thinking ahead: how you can comply today with the aspirations and legislation of the future?

Profitability

There *are* ways to increase productivity, reduce running costs and bring benefits to people, communities and the environment at the same time, but these are not necessarily the obvious tried and tested ways, and so you must spend time and energy seeking out and experimenting with new ways forward.

Running a business isn't easy at the best of times, and if you're trying to adopt ethical principles as well, you may have to make decisions along the way that will have a great impact, but where the way forwards is not clear. Examples might be:

- discovering that, under close scrutiny, a business partner does not live up to your own standards
- you receive a business approach from the 'wrong sort' of customer at a moment when you badly need the work to keep the company viable
- having to choose between a costly, but 'squeaky green', supplier and a much cheaper, but less green, source – especially if the knock-on effect would be that your product becomes more expensive than the competition
- being offered business where the terms attached would make life difficult for your staff (for example, in terms of working hours or pay)

Looking at the options

Often, if you open your mind and engage in some creative thinking around an issue, more options will emerge than you might expect. Doug Hall, a US business creativity expert, suggests that the more different ways you think about a problem, the more likely you are to get ideas. In turn, the greater number of ideas you have, the greater your chance of coming up with the perfect solution.

Here are some thought-starters that could help you move forward:

- Could you **break up** the issue into stages or parts, rather trying to tackle it on all fronts in an instant 'whole-hog' approach?
- What would you do if there was **no risk of failure**? Can any of your plans for that scenario fit the real-life state of play?
- What do other **patterns and trends** suggest?
- What **assumptions** need to be challenged?
- Could a **complete renegotiation** be necessary?
- Could straight talking and a **request for help** in resolving the issue change the dynamics?
- What could **working in partnership** with others bring?

- What might the benefits be of an **extreme position**?
- What if you took a **completely different perspective**? If you didn't know the history and context, what would you do?

Each of the points above could yield several new ways of thinking about the same issue that may shake you out of a rut.

What is best for your business now?

The obvious answer may leap at you just by looking at the options. Or you may need time to think through what the different possibilities mean for you in context. Being clear about your values will help you make decisions that you feel comfortable with.

Values are motivational elements that drive our actions and reactions. They have a natural hierarchy. If we act in a way that is in tune with our values, we feel satisfied. But if we act in a way that is out of alignment with our values, we react with discomfort and experience negative emotions such as anger, shame or disappointment which may be stressful over time.

Your business values

What are the things in business that you feel passionately about? Imagine that you are at the end of your business career and are looking back at what you have done. Write down the things you will be proud that you did or proud that you encouraged. For example:

- Having products and customer service that people rate.
- Making money for yourself and your family.
- Growing the business to a manageable size.
- Keeping informed – learning what's new.
- Taking decisive action.
- Doing right by people – not taking advantage.
- Being trusted.
- Employing local people in good jobs.
- Being willing to explain/train people.

In the same way, make a note of anything that you would regret doing or having encouraged.

Looking at what you have written, what are the important themes? These are your values, so give them a label if you can: it doesn't really matter what words you use so long as they make sense to you. For example, you could use:

- relationships
- fairness

- contributing to local community
- reputation
- control
- profit

Thinking about the bigger picture in this way can sometimes help bring greater clarity to your business conundrum.

Your priorities

As we've seen above, values are motivational elements that drive our actions and reactions. They have a natural hierarchy. If we act in a way that is in tune with our values, giving priority to the right ones for us, we feel satisfied.

To work out the relative importance of these values, you need to work out how they fit together for you. Taking your list of values, ask yourself:

- If I have Number 1, will I have Number 2? For example, in the above case: If I have relationships, will I have fairness?

If the answer is 'Yes', these two are in the correct order. If 'No', try another order until each pair feels right. When you feel comfortable with your order of values, use it as the basis for your priorities and you'll certainly derive benefit from it.

As you work through this exercise you may experience moments of insight about the conundrum you're facing: the answer may, in fact, pop up out of nowhere, meaning that you'll be able to move swiftly to take action. If that doesn't happen, though, don't panic. Don't forget that you are just one part of the system and you might need to get input from close colleagues and partners.

Talk to key partners, suppliers and colleagues

To make the best business decision, you may also need to work out what others' perceptions are and factor these in somehow. If the issue is likely to have wide-reaching consequences, it would be wise for you to find out about the views, priorities and principles of individuals and groups on whom the decision will impact. These stakeholders are a valuable part of your business's system but because they're not involved as much in the everyday details as you are, they may be able to give you some helpful objectivity.

Obviously, you know best how to approach the people you work with closely, but a simple conversation on the phone, online or in person may be all you need. If your business has grown and your budget allows, you could also use:

- focus groups
- employee away-days
- supplier meetings

Whatever route you choose, by connecting with people on the issues, explaining your viewpoint and what might happen if you don't implement a change, you'll be giving them reason to engage with the problem. Communicating your expectations and hopes, in a way that encourages others to do the same, will take you all forward.

You may feel that this approach would be too risky or too difficult with some of the stakeholders in your particular context. You might be thinking: 'I can't discuss such-and-such with Jimmy X or Workgroup Y.' Just extend the invitation. If it's declined, extend it again. When offered a well-prepared invitation to engage in sorting out a problem, people sometimes surprise us by stepping up to the challenge. We'd all rather be part of the solution than tagged as part of the problem.

Preparing for the dialogue
Think about the constituent parts of the problem in advance to clarify your own thinking. Then draft a brief

introduction to the meeting, focusing most of the conversation around a questioning approach:

1. Focus the conversation on the central conundrum.

   > ABC Ltd would like to place a large order for our new widget. However, they've told me that it's going to be used in machinery used in deforestation.

2. Describe why it is a conundrum for you, explaining why (rather than assuming that) your listeners will understand your thinking. Clarify what is at stake as you see it.

   > Not only would our widgets be involved in harming the environment, many local tribespeople would be left homeless.

3. Say clearly that you want to create a way forward with the situation and what your hopes are.

   > ABC does have a range of operations around the world, however, and I think there is a role for us elsewhere. I'd like us to be able to turn this job down without closing the door on future collaborations in another field.

4. Use questions to draw out what other parties feel about the situation and where their

thinking comes from. Explain that you want to know more about their perspective and what it is based on.

5. Ask what you have all learned from the discussion so far and then use questions to take the conversation forward into a creative phase: Where are we now? Where can we go from here? What needs to happen to . . . ? Can we agree to . . .?

Constructing a way forward together with others who are a part of the system improves relationships and enables people to increase the meaning they find in their work. A benefit of investing time in this type of conversation is that it results in a 'stronger ship' that is less likely to come unstuck in the future. Also, it gives you a blueprint for any similar situations that may crop up in the years to come: rather than having to start from a blank slate, you'll be able to use what you learned from this process to get the ball rolling.

Managing ethical risk

Every person in your business brings ethics risk factors of their own into the mix. According to Christopher Bauer, author of *Better Ethics Now* (Aab-Hill Business Books, 2005), these can include:

- financial strain
- relationship difficulties
- emotional distress
- health problems

Each can set the scene for ethics violations simply because each causes us to look for quick fixes, which at some point will include inappropriate ones. You need to monitor your employees' performance systematically in order to recognise, and act against, potential risks to your company's ethical stance.

Many people in business simply rely on their inner voice telling them something isn't right. Leaders rely on other people bringing their concerns to them, or sharing their hunch that something isn't quite as it should be. Having doubts about something is a pretty good early alarm call, but is only as good as the information that is known.

As your business grows, there will be more happening that you are not directly aware of, and you will be relying implicitly or explicitly on the scruples of others. Employees need clear guidelines about how your company's values are to be applied to resolve questions that are not already addressed by specific policies and procedures.

Some topics that you may wish to consider giving guidance on are:

- professional behaviour (meeting commitments, avoiding malpractice or corruption)
- environmental stewardship (looking after the earth and biodiversity)
- economic fairness (not inhibiting the growth of newly developing countries unfairly)
- upholding human rights and respecting others (treating people with dignity and fairness)

Ask staff to discuss any areas that could yield concerns or opportunities in terms of business ethics. Make it clear to them how much you buy into this system, and that you won't be content to let things slide.

Couple this with appropriate supervision to ensure that things actually work out according to your intentions, and adopt a risk prevention strategy. You should regularly be asking questions such as:

- Where might ethical risks arise in our industry?
- Does competition make us more prone to take ethical risks?
- Is there transparency in our decision-making and conduct?
- How dependent are we on our core customers? Does this make us vulnerable?

- How does the structure of the company help or hinder communication and independence?
- Have you made your expectations clear to staff?
- Are your people trained to do a professional job?
- Is ethical behaviour discussed, measured and rewarded?

Finally, be certain to reward (not shoot!) messengers for bringing issues to light. Blowing the whistle can be an incredibly difficult decision to make for anyone, so don't dismiss allegations or complaints before you have investigated them thoroughly.

Further help and resources

The National Centre for Business & Sustainability (NCBS) is a non-profit, values-based consultancy organisation committed to helping individuals and organisations to operate in ways that deliver high levels of environmental and social performance alongside good economic return. For more information, visit: www.thencbs.co.uk

8 'GREENING' YOUR BUSINESS: HOW FAR ARE YOU WILLING TO GO?

Nick Kettles

If everyone in the world consumed at the same rate we do in the UK, we would need three planets to provide the natural resources required to meet demand.[1] So, if we are to 'meet the needs of the present without compromising the ability of future generations to meet their own needs', as the classic definition of sustainability suggests we must, then everyone must play their part, and this includes businesses.

---

[1] Defra- and DTI-funded report on sustainable consumption: 'If You Will, I Will'

As explained in Chapter 1, it's impossible to create an ethical business without its also being a sustainable business and without fulfilling your responsibility to the environment. Small businesses are like individual households when it comes to the environment, in that *individually* they are not going to have a huge impact, but taken as a whole, they're a force to be reckoned with. There are so many small businesses that together they can make as much difference as large corporations.

With consumer demand growing to a critical mass and government legislation making the choice easier, at least from a financial point of view, the question for small businesses today is not whether they will go green, but what shade and how quickly.[2] For those that do, it will quickly become clear this is not a burdensome task, but the key to increased efficiency and substantial cost savings.

Just how sustainable can your business be?

As a model of 'going the extra mile', Acorn House, London's first truly sustainable restaurant, according to *The Times*, represents a wonderful benchmark of

---

[2] Ibid.

sustainability.[3] Yet unless they are willing to offset the carbon impact of their customers' journey to the restaurant, even they might not be able to claim to be 100% sustainable. The fact is that while it's *theoretically* possible to be 100% sustainable as a business, in practice this usually means a large investment up front. For example, for the majority of businesses that do not own their own premises, it's neither practical nor good business to invest in building a new eco-office, which would take a couple of generations to pay for itself.

However, for many, 'greening' their existing business premises to reduce its impact on the environment is both viable and a distinct possibility. You have to start somewhere, and the best place to do that is by making small changes yourself. As you see the tangible results of these changes, your confidence will grow and you'll be ready to do more.

Setting benchmarks and reduction targets

Trewin Restorick, director of Global Action Plan (www.globalactionplan.org.uk), the environmental charity that helps people and organisations make environmental and financial savings, believes that the

---

[3] www.timesonline.co.uk/tol/life_and_style/food_and_drink/giles_coren/article663409.ece

principles of good environmental practice are easier to implement for a small business. In his view, 'It's easier to assess a small business's impact and whether they are meeting all their obligations. Providing the processes are embedded into the organisation from the outset, it's easier to monitor.'

To do this, Global Action Plan say it's necessary to have measurable benchmarks which set ambitious reduction targets, and, moreover, to report openly about those targets and your success in meeting them. Given the time available to a small business, it's advisable to use established road maps in setting these benchmarks and targets.

The main benchmark with which small businesses should be familiar is British Standard 8555 (BS 8555), a generic 'environmental management standard' which attempts to provide a practical framework and objective criteria with which to reduce and manage a company's environmental impact. BS 8555 has been specifically designed to help smaller businesses move towards ISO 14001, an internationally accepted specification for improving environmental management, by following a set of clearly defined steps.

Although it may sound complex, Global Action Plan say, in practice it's actually quite easy, and can save extraordinary amounts of money.

Establishing a baseline

Obviously, the first step is your commitment to take action, and this should start with establishing a baseline for setting in place your environmental management system. In practice, this means making a thorough examination of what you are doing right now as a starting point for setting goals. Every business is different, but questions you must ask include:

- What waste do I create?
- What energy and water do I use?
- What comes into my company? What goes out of my company?
- What do my employees do? What impact does their travel have on the environment?
- How are our products and services transported, and what impact do those routes have?
- How far do our customers have to travel to buy our products or use our services?
- What's our impact on the local community? Do we employ local people? Do we support the community and its charities?

Complying with legal – and other – requirements

Before you set specific targets to improve upon your

baseline, you should examine all the legal requirements you are obliged to meet. This process is essential for the legal status of your business but also to help reset your baseline. Once you are fully compliant, you can set targets about how much further you wish to go.

By far the best place to find out about environmental legislation and requirements is the UK Environmental Agency's Netregs website (www.netregs.gov.uk). This informative and easy-to-navigate site offers guidance for SMEs (small and medium enterprises) on regulations such as the WEEE directive on the responsible disposal of electrical equipment (see page 21) as well as those regulations specific to their sector of industry.

So, if you work in the construction industry, for example, you'll be able to investigate the finer details of the legislation regarding the disposal of asbestos, or how to tackle Japanese knotweed. If you work in the textile industry, on the other hand, you'll find information on the protocols you'll need to meet for the safe disposal of treatment dyes.

Developing objectives, targets and programmes

The next step is to set goals about where you want to be in a year's time. The goals you set will, of course, be relative to the size of your business, but at the very least 'increasing efficiency' and 'reducing costs' should be poiners guiding the way.

There is a plethora of support and information available about how to reduce your environmental impact in each of the key areas below:

Energy use

With the 2001 Climate Change Levy adding some 20% to commercial users' energy bills, there's no more satisfying place to start than examining how you can reduce your electricity use. Inefficient use of office machines costs UK businesses up to a staggering £100 million in electricity every year.

According to the Carbon Trust, leaving a computer on 24/7 costs four times more than if you switch it off at night and weekends; a fluorescent tube uses 500 times more energy if left on for 15 minutes than the energy needed to restart it; while a mid-volume photocopier left on overnight uses enough energy to produce over 1,500 copies. Switching off electrical appliances requires very little effort and should be the foundation stone of establishing good environmental management.

No less effective in reducing costs and your impact on the environment is switching to more energy-efficient light bulbs. While more expensive than standard light bulbs, the energy-efficient variety use at least 75% less energy, and will quickly pay for themselves. The same is true of using energy efficiency 'A' rated electrical appliances, such as refrigerators.

Further energy-saving tips can be found at the Friends of the Earth website www.foe.co.uk/living/forum/ and www.thecarbontrust.co.uk (0800 585794).

If your company has a dedicated IT department responsible for managing your network, then it's worth checking out *Computing Magazine*'s Green Computing campaign, which aims to raise awareness of environmental issues in IT departments (www.computing.co.uk).

Who you buy your electricity from can also have an impact. The website www.ukgreenpower.co.uk is a great resource from which to find out more about buying electricity generated from renewable sources. Indeed, it's possible for your company to produce its *own* energy by installing renewable energy technologies such as ground-source heat pumps or solar panels on-site. In some instances, there are grants available. Investigate the Low Carbon Buildings Programme (LCBP) www.lowcarbonbuildings.org.uk/home or, in Scotland, www.energysavingtrust.org.uk/schri

Recycling
According to the Environment Agency, 75% of the UK's

municipal waste is sent to landfill, 9% is incinerated and only 16% is recycled. This compares with recycling rates of 30–60% common in other European countries.

Businesses are no better. According to Friends of the Earth, 70% of office waste is paper, invariably the kind of high-grade white paper most sought-after for recycling, yet only 15% is actually recycled. Recycling just 1 ton of paper can save 3,700 pounds of lumber and 24,000 gallons of water.[4]

Renia Spong, environmental consultancy manager with Waste Watch Environmental Consultancy (www.wastewatch.org.uk) says: 'Reducing the amount of waste produced in the first place is the most effective way to reduce costs and your organisation's impact on the environment.

'Simple measures such as setting photocopiers and printers to automatically print double-sided and using scrap paper as notepads can literally halve paper consumption and associated purchasing and disposal costs.'[5]

For more tips on recycling, see Chapter 5. And for more information about the disposal of waste specific to your industry, see www.netregs.gov.uk. The Waste &

---

[4]London Recycling.
[5]www.newbuilder.co.uk/newbuilder/NewsFullStory.asp?ID=668

Resources Management Programme (WRAP) (www. wrap.org.uk) also offers information on organisations that collect waste.

Purchasing and procurement

Having started to reduce your energy consumption and to recycle more, you can reduce your impact on the environment still further by only purchasing recycled goods.

Just like the NetRegs and WRAP websites, www.recycledproducts.org.uk is a veritable gateway to suppliers of recycled goods for the small office, companies in the construction, manufacturing and retail sectors, as well as those involved in landscaping, horticulture, agriculture and facilities management.

WRAP will also provide more specific advice to retailers looking to work with their supply lines to minimise waste, reduce packaging and encourage recycling; manufacturers that want to reduce their reliance on the use of virgin materials; and those in the construction industry who wish to be more efficient.

Travel and transport

With congestion charges set to become more widespread, and parking charges increasing, supporting your employees in using either public transport to get to work or car-pooling will have a big effect on your impact on the environment as well as their disposable income. This can become even more efficient if you are willing to discuss car-pooling with employees from neighbouring businesses. The website www.liftshare.com offers great advice on effective ways to share your journey to work.

However, employing local people who can either walk or cycle to work, where possible, will have an even greater impact. One government scheme, Cycle to Work, offers incentives aimed at encouraging employees to use pedal power to get to work, by allowing them to benefit from a long-term loan of bikes and commuting equipment such as lights, locks and panniers completely tax free. More information can be found online at: www.bikeforall.net

How many miles your suppliers clock up in providing you with what you need to run your business should also be a consideration. If you can find a local supplier, then where possible you should use them. Not only will this reduce the impact on the environment your product or service has, but it will also help to support the local economy, which indirectly may mean the employment of people, who will then purchase your product or service.

Recognising this kind of virtuous circle is a very powerful way of developing a plan of action when you are deciding which choices to prioritise. Many of the above suggestions are interdependent, and so it's important to recognise where one simple change to your business can be more effective than many.

Greening working practices

One of the most powerful ways to make a positive impact on the environment is to implement greener working practices. These can reduce the use of transport, and the need for larger, more energy-intensive premises, while also supporting employees in adopting healthier work–life balance practices.

Even if you don't feel comfortable allowing employees to 'tele-work from home', then offering flexible working hours may allow you to reduce electricity costs by making your premises or offices available outside peak hours when electricity is more expensive. For more information, see www.flexibleworking.co.uk.

Implementing and operating an environmental management system

The next step is to implement your plan. By far the most important factor here is allowing your staff to take ownership of your project, and not simply making it a diktat from the top down. Establish a work group or a 'green team' to set in motion the necessary actions and timescales, and put in place the assessment criteria.

Follow up by having regular meetings to communicate what you have achieved to the rest of the organisation. This can help increase buy-in to the project, boost employee morale, and also expand the implementation of the project.

Checking and auditing the environmental management system

The support of a third party is invaluable at this stage, because it offers the necessary objectivity to ensure you haven't compromised in any of the key areas. Indeed, seeking the advice of a third party may just be the best place to start, if following BS 8555 on your own is too dry, overwhelming or time-consuming. Either way, seek the support of a group or organisation, ideally not-for-profit, which is already working in alignment with BS 8555 and ISO 14001.

Envirowise (see Chapter 5; www. envirowise.gov.uk) provides more information on benchmarking. Alternatively, there are a number of regionally based non-profit organisations that can help. For example, the Business & Environment Management Scheme (BEMS) offer their award-winning business support project across the East Midlands and East of England to help businesses deliver more sustainable profits whilst reducing their environmental impact.

Global Action Plan (see page 114) also have regional schemes, including SmartWorks, which focuses on helping businesses throughout London with less than 250 staff, and EnVision, a partnership of experienced environmental organisations across South West England which primarily focuses on helping small businesses in so-called 'Objective 2', or more deprived, areas.

Groups such as these will be able to advise you on how to report your success, year on year, to the public, as well as how to work towards full ISO 14001 accreditation.

Industry marques and accreditation

It's worth, too, looking to see if there are any industry marques or accreditation schemes dedicated to making the 'greening' process more accessible and applicable to the specific needs of your industry or sector.

One of the best examples of this is the Green Tourism Business Scheme (www.green-business.co.uk). This offers three awards (bronze, silver and gold) to hotels, bed and breakfasts, tour operators and other companies involved in the holiday business that meet certain criteria. What started out as a niche project, ten years ago, is growing rapidly, with over 1,200 members across the UK, including some larger hotel chains with many premises.

Where accreditation schemes like this are different is that they can offer bespoke advice with case studies that match industries' specific needs, including how to market the environmental message to the customer. They are also more aspirational than more paper-trail-based schemes, and as they perpetuate themselves can become a growing network of industry good practice.

Andrea Nicholas, Managing Director of Green Business UK Ltd, the non-profit organisation which runs the Green Tourism Business Scheme, says: 'It has come to the point where in some areas of the country, if you haven't got a green label, then you are missing out on business. There is one area where one local tourism website took the green logo off their website, because the green businesses were getting too much business. Thankfully, it got put back on.'

However, while the Green Tourism Scheme is a shining example of what can be done, there are still far too few other industries that are following suit. So, providing you have the time, energy and inclination, an opportunity exists for your business to become a benchmark for the whole industry.

9 ETHICAL BANKING AND FINANCE

Nick Kettles

> Banking ethically isn't just about choosing a bank with the right credentials. If you want your ethical policy to be truly effective, you need to commit to being rigorous about every financial transaction or decision that you make. Many of these decisions will just be good common sense, but others will require you to go the extra mile if you want to be sure your money works for change and not against it.

Loans and accounts

For ethically inspired businesses seeking funding to get up and running, choosing which bank to approach for a loan can be instrumental to the business's future success. Contacting a bank such as Triodos (www.triodos.co.uk), for example, which specialises in lending money to socially and environmentally inspired businesses, means you will benefit from their knowledge and experience of the sector over and above the money they loan you.

Some banks or building societies have an expertise in a specific area, so it's worth researching beyond the most obvious ethical candidates to see if you can match your project precisely to an institution's lending experience. The West Yorkshire-based Ecology Building Society (www.ecologybuildingsociety.co.uk), for instance, specialises in lending to landlords, housing co-operatives and housing associations, as well as other commercial ventures; the Unity Trust Bank (www.unity.uk.com) has a track record of supporting not-for-profit organisations.

Ethically inspired banks are not without the ability to raise larger sums of capital, too. In 2006, Triodos raised £250,000 of ordinary equity investment from four private investors for Natural Building Technologies (NBT), a technical sales and product development business bringing a new generation of building materials and designs to the mainstream market. They also acted as lead advisers on Cafédirect's (www.cafedirect.co.uk) successful share issue in 2004, which raised £5 million from thousands of private investors, and helped to take the company to the next stage in its development.

However, depending on whom you approach – whether to apply for a loan or simply to open an account – your ethical policy may get put to the test even before you've started up. To illustrate, the Co-operative Bank (www.co-operativebank.co.uk) requires all business customers to complete a questionnaire, which is then assessed against the bank's own ethical policy. If a conflict is identified, the application is passed to the bank's Ethical Policy Unit, where the business is reviewed against a series of policy statements and the 1,700-plus case studies held on file. The most recent figures available show that in 2002 the bank declined 29% of businesses referred to its Ethical Policy Unit. And in 2005 alone, the Co-operative turned away business worth more than £10 million.

However, while the Co-operative is known for being at the leading edge of ethical finance, each business is free to decide the focus of its ethical policy, and how to implement it. If, for example, social inclusion is central to your business's ethical policy, then banking with Barclays might be the right choice for you. In recent years, they have been active in supporting credit unions and community development finance institutions (CDFIs), which provide affordable personal or business credit to financially excluded people, who often fall prey to high interest rate charges from loan sharks operating in their communities.

Other financial products

Like any other type of consumer, business customers can be instrumental in shaping the market for other financial products.

Savings

If it is your policy to save for your tax bill in advance, you may want to consider depositing that money in the Charity Bank (the UK's only not-for-profit bank) before you give it to the taxman. This bank has to date provided affordable loans totalling more than £55 million to over 500 charitable organisations that do not have easy access to mainstream lending. For more information, visit www.charitybank.org or call them on 01732 774040.

Insurance

While the insurance industry doesn't immediately leap to mind as being at the vanguard of change, there are some companies that do recognise that they can be a vehicle for sustainable development. For example, Naturesave Policies Ltd (www.naturesave.co.uk) places 10% of all its personal insurance premiums into a fund to benefit environmental and conservationist projects. It also offers a free environmental performance review for all its commercial clients as well as financial assistance to its SME clients to help them offset their carbon emissions.

Pensions

As a result of the many pension scandals that have come to light in the last few years, the UK government's intention is for employers to become more involved in the promotion and administration of pension payments. If your employees make payroll deductions to their pension scheme, you could explain to them that there are more than 70 ethical funds in the UK into which they could invest. Obviously, expert advice should be sought to help your employees make the right choice. There are a number of so-called ethical financial advisers, such as Ethical Investor Group (www.ethicalinvestors.co.uk), who claim they will be happy to undertake a pension review on behalf of ethical employers.

If all staff agreed to pay into the same fund, you could even make a saving yourself, as you'd have fewer direct debit mandate charges to cover.

Managing payments to your business

The government-backed Better Payment Practice Campaign (BPPC) (www.payontime.co.uk) estimates that small businesses lose *billions* of pounds every year as a result of late and unpaid invoices; some are even made bankrupt as a result. Late payment of invoices is not only unethical, but also an unhealthy business practice. It can damage your reputation with suppliers, as well as weaken the economy as a whole by constricting growth. The flow of cash in the economy is supposed to cascade, not trickle, down the chain of suppliers, starting with large organisations. Unfortunately, only one-third of PLCs pay their bills within 30 days, and over four years there has been no improvement in their average payment times.[1]

But the part small businesses play in the economy is no less important. So, if you've taken the time to formulate an ethical policy based on honesty and integrity, then you should offer nothing less in your willingness to meet your suppliers' terms and conditions and pay bills promptly.

At all times, payment terms should be based on clear, open communication; if a supplier can only offer you terms that you know you will be unable to meet, then you simply should not accept them. By the same token, having an ethical policy which states who you will and won't work with doesn't mean that you

---

[1]Source: Companies House 2003.

shouldn't check out your customers' ability to pay, especially if your business offers credit: it's important that you know who you are offering it to. For all prospective customers – even if they've been referred by someone you know – have a full credit check run on them. This will reveal any recent county court judgments (CCJs) that have been served on a business for late payment. You could also contact Companies House and ask to look at their accounts (www.companieshouse.gov.uk).

Even if the prospective customer does have a good credit rating, don't be afraid to ask for part-payment in advance until you're happy that you can trust the other party. So that everyone is clear about what the terms of payment are, always make sure that you confirm the terms in writing, preferably supported by a signed contract. According to the Better Payment Practice Group (BPPG), one in three companies do not bother to do this.

Similarly, if a customer does default on a payment, you should equally be willing to use the law to obtain the money you're owed. There are a number of specialised schemes, such as the aforementioned BPPG and Prompt Payer (www.promptpayer.co.uk), which provide detailed advice on issues such as:

■ **legislation relating to charging interest on late payers**

- negotiating with them
- seeing through common excuses used to delay payment still further
- taking court action, if necessary

Although it can be a slow process, the law is on your side. Seeking a CCJ is the correct course of action for most business-to-business transactions and will, in the majority of cases, elicit payment. CCJs are like a black mark for a business, forewarning others of their poor payment history, and can only be removed if payment is made within the time set by the court from the date of the judgment.

Prompt Payer and the BPPG also offer registers and pledges you can sign to show your commitment to paying on time. While they do not have any force in law, they will forewarn potential customers that defaulting on a payment will not be ignored.

But there are other ways to ease your business's cash flow without compromising your ethical policy. Local Exchange Trading Schemes (LETS) or TimeBanks (part of the TimeBank UK project; find out more at: www.timebank.org.uk) are community-based networks in which individuals, voluntary groups and small businesses can exchange goods and services with one another, without the need for money. A system of credits is used, which means that direct exchanges do not have to be made.

Participating in such schemes can help members of the community access your goods and services without the need for money, while also allowing you to benefit from goods and services such as tool or equipment hire, childcare, repairs or transport, which would otherwise make a sizeable dent in your business expenditure.

Sharing wealth

If your business is committed to ethical practices in terms of fair business, and committed to Fairtrade principles and employment practices, you will already be doing much to ensure a better redistribution of wealth in the world. There are, however, ways in which you can share wealth *within* your organisation. Providing a profit share, or allowing your employees to take a stake in your company as shareholders, can enhance their motivation considerably. Indeed, business research does show that employee share ownership can have a positive effect on company performance, by reducing feelings of 'us and them' towards management, reducing the propensity to quit and encouraging a greater awareness of colleagues' work behaviour.

Setting up a workers' co-operative, either as a new

business or by transforming the organisational structure of an existing business, is another option. This takes things one step further than share ownership, by making your employees part-owners of the company. In the simplest terms, this means they will be sharing responsibility for both the assets of the company and decision-making about its future.

Amongst many sources of help, local Business Links or the Industrial Common Ownership Movement (ICOM) section of Co-operatives UK (www.euro-social-economy.org.uk/icom) can advise which co-operative organisational structure would be right for your company.

How you choose to manage your money as a business is one of the most powerful statements you can make about your commitment to ethical working. Ultimately, the choices you make about money will reveal just how far you are willing to go in the implementation of your ethical policy.

> For a complete list of ethical banks, check out the *Guide to Responsible Banking*, published by the Ethical Investment Research Service (EIRIS). You can contact them online at www.eiris.org.uk or by phone on 020 7840 5700.

Carry Somers

The background

Pachacuti means 'world upside-down' in the Quechua language and describes my aim to show that it *can* be possible to run a successful clothing business which benefits the producers and is environmentally sustainable.

I set up the company in 1992 after I had finished an MA in Native American Studies. On a research trip to Ecuador, I was shocked by the inequitable trading patterns, where intermediaries made all the profits. After

VIEWPOINT

hearing how two co-operatives had been intimidated by powerful middlemen and had even been affected by arson, I decided to act and gave them the financial resources to buy raw materials in bulk. I had no background in design, but produced a series of knitwear patterns based on cave art in the region which proved so popular that they sold out in six weeks. Seeing the tangible difference this made to the producers' livelihoods encouraged me to give up my PhD and concentrate on improving the lives of more producer groups in the Andean region.

The business has grown rapidly ever since, and we supply shops and mail order catalogues all over the world; our clients include The Conran Shop, Fenwicks and the National Trust catalogue.

We work with a variety of producers in Latin America and are proud to support communities such as the only women's panama hat association in Ecuador, providing the principal income for over 200 weavers. Our commitment grows regularly, however: in June 2007, I began working with a new co-operative which has just started to export and will be buying their entire production capacity! I also work with over 400 embroiderers, tailors, knitters and milliners who participate in co-operatives, community groups and mother's clubs throughout the Andean region.

Obviously, fair trade means ensuring that my producers receive excellent remuneration for their work, sometimes as much as double the price they would get from selling to an intermediary. I also try to go the extra mile, however, and actively work to improve working conditions, empower female workers and try to ensure sustainability through the reduced use of chemicals and the use of rainforest-friendly buttons.

I've found that our customers are interested in the whole package: our principles, the products we offer, how individual each piece is, and so on. They're often surprised by how involved I am, but I genuinely do take part in each stage of the production process, from design up.

The challenges

I find that the most challenging parts of the job are staying on top of production and managing logistics: it can be nerve-racking not knowing what might happen while the products are en route. For example, heavy rain can interrupt deliveries, breakages can happen and so on, and at times it can feel as if it's all getting out of control. I've even known shipments to 'disappear', only to turn up safely a few weeks later!

For simplicity, all the logistics are trafficked via me. (The paperwork does get a bit tedious, but I know it's

VIEWPOINT

essential and like to do it myself so that I keep on top of everything.) To a large extent, we're dependent on our producers for updates on the progress of orders, and given their remote location that can be tricky. Some of them do have phones, but they're not always that good at replying. In other cases, I've been known to leave messages at petrol stations for people to pick up next time they fill up, or leave messages at family members' houses.

I get such a lot out of running the business, despite the many responsibilities, and find it very rewarding to visit my producers in Ecuador. The trips always remind me how much there is to do, and they renew my sense of purpose. For example, even small things, like offering a bonus on All Saints' Day to the workers, or offering an extra ten pensions for those who are ready to retire, have a massive impact. We've even paid into a fund so that all workers can draw out money for funerals of family members. The sums involved seem very small to us, but mean a great deal to the workers. In many cases, the money actually keeps them alive: they have no State support, and if they have no relatives to look after them, without our pension scheme they would be left to fend for themselves in their old age.

Future projects

My daughter Sienna was the inspiration behind our new business, which supplies organic Fairtrade school uniforms. Most uniforms these days are coated in Teflon, a component of which is thought to be a carcinogen, whilst schoolwear labelled as 'Easy Care' has been found to contain high levels of formaldehyde. My daughter had heard about this and refused to wear them. We just couldn't find any uniforms that didn't have this covering, so we developed our own brand of them for her.

The new business, Clean Slate, is barely a year old (www. cleanslateclothing.co.uk). The set-up was difficult stock-wise, in that 25% of the stock arrived wrongly sized! It cost us thousands of pounds. The products have been very well received and at the time of writing we're getting lots of orders for our organic summer dresses. There has been a great deal of interest, particularly from parents whose children have eczema or other allergies and who have previously found it very hard to find uniforms which are not treated with chemicals.

Nick Kettles

Nick Kettles is a freelance writer and brand consultant. In this Viewpoint, he explains how formulating an ethical policy marked a turning point for his company, from which new opportunities and growth have developed.

The back story

It's always been important to me to work with honesty and integrity, and that aspect of business life was reinforced when my partner and I encountered clients who ripped us off. To cut a long story short, one refused to pay us after we'd completed work for them. After our credit terms had expired, we contacted them to discuss how they were going to pay us, but they simply ignored our calls. After some time, they finally admitted they were waiting for payment from a customer before they could pay us, but, as we pointed out, that wasn't our fault: it was their responsibility to manage their cash-flow better, not ours.

After more broken promises, we eventually decided to take them to court. It is a potentially long and

142

expensive process, yes, but I felt that we had to do it on principle. They were furious, and yet it turned out that they already had a county court judgment (CCJ) against them for non-payment (a tip: always check a potential new customer's credit rating before you agree to work with them. It would have saved us a lot of time and effort in this case, and we certainly make a point of doing it now). However, once the court order had gone through, they did play ball, and after an initial payment of half the amount owing, we agreed a payment plan. Over time they underwent a bit of a sea change and admitted their mistake, and even apologised to us. It took us 11 months from issuing the original invoice to be paid in full. Because of their change in attitude, I asked the court to remove the CCJ against them in the end, too.

In another incident, we discovered that a previous client was actively supporting the reinstatement of commercial whaling at the time we had worked for them. Being active supporters of cetacean preservation, we were devastated to discover this. We realised that if we had had an ethical policy, stating who we were and were not happy to work with, and under what terms, we would not have taken the work on in the first place.

It was a watershed moment, and we decided that

from that point on we'd be very clear about who we would work with (and how), and that our customers would have to buy in to that, rather than the other way round. We were scared at first at the possibility of having to turn work away, of course, but we felt so strongly about it that it was something we felt we had to see through.

The profits/ethics conundrum

People do worry about how a company can be profitable *and* ethical, as if one precludes the other. How can I be both? Yet in spite of the fact that many business practices are formed around the central theme of 'how can I get one over on you?', people do actually hear you when you say something new and are pleased by other messages. I think increasingly people are tired of the way marketers speak to them, and so they respond well to sincerity.

However, having an ethical policy shouldn't stop you from being pragmatic and willing to change the products and services you offer, if the feedback you get from customers reveals a valid point.

For example, our company, NewMythCreate, was a network of freelance writers and consultants. After formulating our ethical policy, we looked at our marketing and took out a Google Ads campaign focusing on securing 'green business', but it didn't have the impact we were looking for. We had literally thousands of click-throughs, but they didn't translate into much new business.

We took a really hard look at what we were doing, and realised we were trying to do too much under one umbrella. For example, I used to do copywriting and brand consultancy, and subcontract and manage work for other writers, all marketed from the same website. Even though our ethical policy felt good to us, it wasn't central to what we did, or how we came across.

So, we decided to split the different elements of the business up, to provide more clarity. I now promote my work as a copywriter independently (having dropped the freelancers network, where margins were too tight); provide ethical brand consultancy and '*refreshingly honest marketing*', through a new venture, BrandBeautiful; and have 'rebirthed' the shell of NewMythCreate into an e-publishing company.

With this new clarity in how we are marketing ourselves, our ethical policy is now making it easier to get work from people who actively want to work with a business operating on those lines. If potential clients don't meet it, and/or they're not willing to work with us in a way that we feel comfortable with, we go our separate ways.

VIEWPOINT

It's certainly been the toughest lesson we've had to learn, but it's been the healthiest, as it's helped us to sharpen our focus, and we hope the business will be stronger for it too.

Working for myself? It's always exciting. I like being self-employed and love the autonomy in particular. The need to constantly sell yourself requires a lot of motivation, of course, but if you stick with it the rewards are great.

Lesley Somers

Lesley Somers is the founder of The Flame Tree, a Fairtrade enterprise with roots in the UK and Ghana. The Flame Tree sells a range of craft products and clothing produced in northern Ghana by women who benefit from the development opportunity, and we also support adult literacy projects in the area. The business's other arm functions in Tottenham, north London, where it is committed to training and creating opportunities for young people and creating links between them and the community in Ghana.

Here Lesley explains what prompted her to start her business, and what gave rise to its unusual remit.

VIEWPOINT

I used to work for an NGO, and as part of my role there I took young people post-GCSE or studying at A level on trips for a short-term experience of life in Africa. I had the opportunity to visit Togo and Ghana and got a sense of the immense difference between our lifestyle and that of the people there. These trips opened my eyes to some of the real differences, and the real needs.

VIEWPOINT

In 2002, I decided to embark on a degree in African Studies and Development Studies at SOAS (the School of Oriental and African Studies) in London. I was especially interested in literacy issues in the West African region and, as part of my module on that subject, returned to Ghana for three weeks to do my thesis. While I was there, I noticed a massive need to improve the literacy levels amongst adults – most efforts to improve literacy in the region focus on children as part of the UN's Millennium Development Goals (www.un.org/millenniumgoals), so they are getting some help, but a generation had been missed. Where we are based, a staggering 80% of women are unable to read.

There was little opportunity for adults to gain those skills, and because there were few primary school teachers who had been trained to teach in the local language, they'd slipped through the net. The women I met had plenty of energy and drive but little opportunity to learn or to maximise their skills. I wondered what I could do, and was prompted by the experience I'd gained from working for my daughter, Carry, at Pachacuti (see page 137), selling her Fairtrade handicrafts at various shows and events during the summer hols.

I'd enjoyed that a great deal, and decided to set up my business, The Flame Tree, as a community interest company. We have shareholders and they're behind us every step of the way.

The Flame Tree approach

The Flame Tree has a two-pronged approach, if you like. In Ghana, we operate as a workers' co-operative, producing Fairtrade batik, basketwork, beads and woven cloth. We offer our workers literacy classes that they can attend before they start sewing. Being able to learn together is a great incentive and help for them, and we have funded training to equip the co-operative with what they need to produce good-quality handicrafts. We're just based in towns at the moment, but we're hoping to spread our work to the villages soon too so that more people can benefit from the opportunity for development and the literacy programmes.

The other side of the business involves working with young people in north London. I live in Tottenham from choice. I used to live in a rural community in Devon, but I wasn't ready to retire and wanted to throw myself back in! I relocated to Tottenham to bring me near to my studies, and I love it here — it's completely unpretentious, real and friendly, despite the challenges facing the community.

We very much want to include the community in our business. Our aim is to equip young people with the

VIEWPOINT

VIEWPOINT

skills they need to succeed, encourage them and give them the ability to see it through. It can be very hard for them when the reality of job opportunity doesn't match up to the expectations of life they've received at home, school or through various leisure activities. There are limited slots where they can succeed and be appreciated, but that's where we hope The Flame Tree can help in the future. We're hoping to centre the business on one of the local estates, so at the moment we're establishing what the community's needs are and how we can then work in partnership to deliver the right skills. We also want to build links between the two areas we work with. It will take time to get that aspect right: as you'd imagine, some things just don't 'translate', which means that we need to constantly rethink, rework and realign to make sure that things work from one community to another.

We're not as engaged with the community in Tottenham as much as we'd like yet, but we're keen to train and equip people to take the business forward. It's incredibly exciting to see young people develop and achieve — I'll be ready to move on when they're ready to take over!

INDEX